GLOBAL HERMENEUTICS?

Society of Biblical Literature

International Voices in Biblical Studies

General Editors
Louis C. Jonker and Monica J. Melanchthon

Number 1
GLOBAL HERMENEUTICS?
Reflections and Consequences

GLOBAL HERMENEUTICS?
Reflections and Consequences

Edited by
Knut Holter and Louis C. Jonker

Society of Biblical Literature
Atlanta

Copyright © 2010 by the Society of Biblical Literature

All rights reserved. No part of this work may be reproduced or published in print form except with permission from the publisher. Individuals are free to copy, distribute, and transmit the work in whole or in part by electronic means or by means of any information or retrieval system under the following conditions: (1) they must include with the work notice of ownership of the copyright by the Society of Biblical Literature; (2) they may not use the work for commercial purposes; and (3) they may not alter, transform, or build upon the work. Requests for permission should be addressed in writing to the Rights and Permissions Office, Society of Biblical Literature, 825 Houston Mill Road, Atlanta, GA 30329, USA.

Library of Congress Cataloging-in-Publication Data

International Organization for the Study of the Old Testament. Congress (19th : 2007 : Ljubljana, Slovenia)
  Global hermeneutics? : reflections and consequences / edited by Knut Holter and Louis C. Jonker.
      p. cm. — (Society of Biblical Literature international voices in biblical studies ; v. 1)
  Includes bibliographical references (p.   ).
  ISBN 978-1-58983-477-4 (electronic publication) — ISBN 978-1-58983-593-1 (pbk : alk. paper)
  1. Bible. O.T.—Hermeneutics—Congresses. 2. Globalization—Religious aspects—Christianity—Congresses. I. Holter, Knut, 1958- II. Jonker, Louis C. III. Title.
  BS476.I633 2007
  221.601—dc22
                             2010007393

Table of Contents

Introduction vii
List of Contributors ix

PART I: CONTEXT 1
GEOGRAPHICAL AND INSTITUTIONAL ASPECTS OF GLOBAL OLD TESTAMENT STUDIES
Knut Holter 3

PART II: CASE STUDIES 15
HERMENEUTICAL PERSPECTIVES ON VIOLENCE AGAINST WOMEN AND ON DIVINE VIOLENCE IN GERMAN-SPEAKING OLD TESTAMENT EXEGESIS
Gerlinde Baumann 17
LAND IN THE OLD TESTAMENT: HERMENEUTICS FROM LATIN AMERICA
Roy H. May, Jr. 25
READING THE OLD TESTAMENT FROM A NIGERIAN BACKGROUND: A WOMAN'S PERSPECTIVE
Mary Jerome Obiorah 35

PART III: CONSEQUENCES 45
THE GLOBAL CONTEXT AND ITS CONSEQUENCES FOR OLD TESTAMENT INTERPRETATION
Louis C. Jonker 47
THE GLOBAL CONTEXT AND ITS CONSEQUENCES FOR OLD TESTAMENT TRANSLATION
Aloo Mojola 57

PART IV: AFTERWORD 83
WHEN BIBLICAL SCHOLARS TALK ABOUT "GLOBAL" BIBLICAL INTERPRETATION
Knut Holter 85

Introduction

The XIXth Congress of the International Organisation for the Study of the Old Testament (IOSOT) was held in Ljubljana, Slovenia from 15–20 July 2007. It was the first time that this esteemed international Old Testament society held its meeting in Eastern Europe. Except for the 1986 meeting in Jerusalem, all the previous seventeen meetings took place in Western Europe.

The President of the IOSOT during the term 2004–2007 was Prof. Jože Krašovec, a professor in Biblical Studies at the Theological Faculty in Ljubljana. His firm commitment to making this conference accessible to particularly Eastern European scholars was complemented by his invitation to Prof. Dr. Knut Holter to put together a special session on "Global Biblical Hermeneutics", which would be scheduled as part of the programme. His desire was that reflection on the impact of the global world on our biblical interpretative endeavours should be stimulated by this special session.

The papers included in this volume, the first proceedings in the newly-established International Voices in Biblical Studies (an initiative of the International Cooperation Initiative of the Society of Biblical Literature), are the deliberations of a handful of international scholars who participated in, and contributed to, the special seminar at the Ljubljana IOSOT conference. They are offered here as a first volume in the new publication series, since this new series has the same objective as the Ljubljana session, namely to stimulate reflection on biblical hermeneutics on a global scale.

The volume covers three aspects in different sections, reflecting the structure of the original session at the Ljubljana conference. Firstly, the paper by Prof. Knut Holter provides an overview of the geographical and institutional context of our global hermeneutical endeavours. A second section offers some case studies from different parts of the world. Dr. Gerlinde Baumann from Germany grapples with the position of women and violence in biblical interpretation, Prof. Roy May addresses the issue of land in biblical interpretation in Latin America, and Prof. Mary Jerome Obiorah engages with women readers of the Bible in her Nigerian context. The third section explores the consequences of the global hermeneutical context for biblical interpretation (particularly in the paper by Prof. Louis Jonker) and Bible translation (in the contribution from Dr. Aloo Mojola). Since all scholars who participated in the mentioned conference session are specializing in Old Testament / Hebrew Bible the illustrative materials are mainly taken from the Old Testament.

When one reads the contributions in these first three sections, one becomes aware of the fact that the global context or globalization as such, is valued in different ways. In some papers (particularly those of Holter, Baumann, Obiorah and Jonker) globalization is described very positively as the context that provides the opportunity to challenge contexts of oppression, and to invite different methodological approaches and ideological viewpoints to a liminal space of communality and inter-contextuality. In other essays (such as those of May and Mojola) globalization is closely associated with the project of imperialism. There, a negative evaluation of globalization is given. When biblical scholars talk about globalization some dissonances can be detected.

In an afterword Prof. Knut Holter therefore reflects on why this might be. He comes to the conclusion that contemporary biblical interpretation is part of the modern globalization project from at least two perspectives: The first perspective acknowledges the fact that we today face a global distribution of communities that interpret the Bible, whereas the second perspective acknowledges—and in some cases tries to counteract—the fact that these globally distributed interpretative communities tend to prolong the traditionally Western hegemony of biblical interpretation.

The papers included in this volume have been peer-reviewed by two internationally renowned scholars in the field. Our gratitude goes to them for helping to ensure the academic quality of this work, as well as to the contributors who made their work available for publication in this volume.

KNUT HOLTER
LOUIS JONKER

List of Contributors

DR. GERLINDE BAUMANN
Privatdozentin, Fachgebiet Altes Testament, Fachbereich Evangelische Theologie, Philipps-University of Marburg, Marburg, Germany
Research Fellow, Department of Biblical and Religious Studies, Faculty of Theology, University of Pretoria, Pretoria, South Africa
(baumann@staff.uni-marburg.de)

PROF. DR. KNUT HOLTER
Department of Biblical Studies, School of Mission and Theology, Stavanger, Norway
Professor Extraordinaire, Department Old and New Testament, Faculty of Theology, University of Stellenbosch, Stellenbosch, South Africa
(knut.holter@mhs.no)

PROF. DR. LOUIS C. JONKER
Department Old and New Testament, Faculty of Theology, University of Stellenbosch, Stellenbosch, South Africa
(lcj@sun.ac.za)

PROF. DR. ROY H. MAY, JR.
Latin American Biblical University, San José, Costa Rica
(roymay@ubila.net)

DR. ALOO MOJOLA
United Bible Societies, Dodoma, Kenya
(mojola@maf.or.ke)

PROF. DR. MARY JEROME OBIORAH
Department of Religion, University of Nigeria, Nsukka, Nigeria
(mjchukwu@yahoo.co.uk)

Part I

CONTEXT

Geographical and Institutional Aspects of Global Old Testament Studies

KNUT HOLTER

INTRODUCTION

Academic studies of the Old Testament—as we know this field within our guild, the International Organisation for the Study of the Old Testament (IOSOT)—are for most practical purposes a northern, theological enterprise.

First, it is mainly a northern enterprise, simply because most of us are northerners. We call ourselves an international guild, and when we interact—by visiting each other, sending students to each other or doing research together—we refer to this as 'internationalisation' in our annual institutional reports. Still, it is mainly a northern internationalisation, as most of us come from—and therefore express and reflect the concerns of—the North Atlantic or North Mediterranean. As far as IOSOT is concerned, it is mainly a European organisation, as pointed out at our congress in Oslo nine years ago by David J. A. Clines. After a survey of participants and paper readers in the IOSOT congresses between 1953 and 1998, he concludes that the organisation will have to decide whether to rename itself a European organisation or to take steps to become what its traditional name actually suggests, a more representatively international organisation.[1]

Second, academic Old Testament studies—again, as we know this within the IOSOT—are mainly a theological enterprise. Certainly, not all of us consider ourselves theologians. And our guild has members whose institutional framework is not a faculty of theology, but rather faculties of arts or social sciences, with their various departments of Ancient Near Eastern languages, linguistics, literature, religious studies, or even biblical studies. Still, the majority of the guild members work in institutional frameworks of theology, that is, Christian theology. This fact explains the relatively high number of Old Testament scholars compared to that of specialists in other classical religious texts, and it also explains why a theologically biased name like the "International Organisation for the Study of the Old Testament" has survived up until today.

My message here is that the first of these two points, the predominantly northern context of academic Old Testament studies, will soon be history, whereas

---

[1] See D. J. A. Clines, "From Copenhagen to Oslo: What has (and has not) happened at congresses of the IOSOT," in *On the Way to the Postmodern: Old Testament Essays, 1967–1998. Volume I.* (ed. D. J. A. Clines; Sheffield; JSOT.S 292; Sheffield Academic Press, 1998), 194–221.

the second point, the—institutionally speaking—theological context of academic Old Testament studies will continue to play an important role. I will argue that we today are able to see how the two develop in parallel. In the same way as Christianity throughout the twentieth and twenty-first centuries is gradually becoming a religion of the Global South, so too are theological and biblical studies gradually becoming southern academic enterprises. The consequence as far as our guild is concerned is that our traditional northern concepts of Old Testament studies will eventually have to be balanced by more southern concepts, as we are heading towards a more global Old Testament studies. This was the rationale behind the organising of a seminar on global biblical hermeneutics in the midst of a typically northern organisation like the IOSOT. The seminar was divided into three parts: Contexts, Cases and Consequences. My own contribution deals with the question of contexts, and it is an attempt at discussing some geographical and institutional aspects of a new and global Old Testament studies in relation to its traditional northern location.[2]

GEOGRAPHICAL ASPECTS

Let me start with some geographical aspects. Proceeding from the observation that Old Testament studies is an academic discipline mainly to be found in Christian theological contexts, I will outline today's global geography as far as Christianity or church membership is concerned. And I will do this by presenting two statistical tables, built on the research of David B. Barrett and Todd M. Johnson at the Center for the Study of Global Christianity, South Hamilton, Mass. in the USA.[3]

---

[2] The literature on biblical interpretation in global contexts is rapidly growing. See e.g. P. Jenkins, *The New Faces of Christianity: Believing the Bible in the Global South* (Oxford: Oxford University Press, 2006); H. Räisänen *et al.* (eds.), *Reading the Bible in the Global Village: Helsinki* (Atlanta: Society of Biblical Literature, 2000); F. F. Segovia, *Decolonizing Biblical Studies: A View From the Margin* (Maryknoll: Orbis, 2000); J. R. Levison and P. Pope-Levison, *Return to Babel: Global Perspectives on the Bible* (Louisville: Westminster John Knox, 1999); R. S. Sugirtharajah, "The Bible and Postcolonialism 1," in *The Postcolonial Bible* (ed. R. S. Sugirtharajah; Sheffield: Sheffield Academic Press, 1998); R. S. Sugirtharajah, "The Bible and Postcolonialism 2," in *Vernacular Hermeneutics* (ed. R. S. Sugirtharajah; Sheffield: Sheffield Academic Press, 1999).

[3] See T. M. Johnson, "Christianity in global context: Trends and statistics" (http://pewforum.org/events/051805/global-christianity.pdf (accessed 2007-06-29)). See also D. B. Barrett, G. T. Kurian and T. M. Johnson (eds.), *World Christian Encyclopedia: A Comparative Survey of Churches and Religions in the Modern World*. Vols. *I and II* (Oxford: Oxford University Press, 2001); D. B. Barrett and T. M. Johnson (eds.), *World Christian Trends AD 30–AD 2200: Interpreting the Annual Christian Megacensus* (Pasadena: William Carey Library, 2001).

The first set of tables outlines the global distribution of church members by United Nations regions:

	1900	1970	2005	2025
Africa	10	143	411	621
Asia	22	101	351	503
Europe	381	492	553	535
S Amer	62	269	517	629
N Amer	79	212	275	306
Oceania	5	18	26	30
Total	558	1,234	2,134	2,626

Million church members

	1900	1970	2005	2025
Africa	9	40	46	48
Asia	2	5	9	11
Europe	95	75	76	77
S Amer	95	95	93	92
N Amer	97	91	83	78
Oceania	78	93	80	76
Total	35	33	33	33

Percentage church members

	1900	1970	2005	2025
Africa	2	12	19	24
Asia	4	8	17	19
Europe	68	40	26	20
S Amer	11	22	24	24
N Amer	14	17	13	12
Oceania	1	1	1	1
Total	100	100	100	100

Percentage of all church members

This set of tables demonstrates how the church throughout the twentieth century gradually moved towards the south. I will not embark on any attempt at explaining the cultural and demographic background of this development; rather, I will restrict myself to commenting briefly upon some of the major trends. And these major trends should be quite easy to observe; the figures show a significant development of twentieth and early twenty-first centuries Christianity leaving its traditional northern context to become a religion of the Global South.

We notice that in 1900 only 2% of the total number of church members lived in Africa, 4% in Asia and 11% in South America, whereas as many as 86% lived in Europe. In 1970 the European percentage of the total number of church members had declined to 40%, whereas it had grown in Africa from 2% to 12%, in Asia from 4% to 8%, and in South America from 11% to 17%. That is, whereas Africa, Asia and South America all together had only a quarter of the European figures in 1900, they were equal in 1970. This development continued throughout the latter decades of the twentieth century. In 2005 the European percentage of the total number of church members had been reduced to 26%, whereas the African percentage had grown to 19%, the Asian to 17% and the South American to 24%. In other words, in one generation—from 1970 to 2005—the global distribution of church members changed from a situation where Europe, on the one hand, and Africa, Asia and South America together, on the other, were approximately equal, to a situation where the latter three have more than double the number of church members compared to Europe. And if we look into the near future at 2025 we see that each of the three southern regions—Africa with 24% of the total number of church members, Asia with 19% and South America with 24%—levels the European 20%. And note that the 2025 figures are not based on pious hopes for a worldwide Christian revival; they reflect a status quo as far as the percentage of church members in each region is concerned. What the figures do take into account, however, are the differences as far as the demographic developments in south and north are concerned.

The figures of the global distribution of church members by regions should be broken down to figures by countries, and so the next table is a kind of *top ten* list, surveying the development of the ten countries which have the highest number of church members (abbr. 'cm').

1900		1970		2005		2025	
Country	Mill cm	Country	Mill cm	Country	Mill cm	Country	Mill cm
USA	73	USA	191	USA	251	USA	280
Russia	62	Brazil	92	Brazil	167	Brazil	193
Germany	42	Germany	70	China	111	China	174
France	41	Russia	50	Mexico	102	Mexico	123
Britain	37	Mexico	50	Russia	84	India	107
Italy	33	Britain	48	Philippines	74	Philippines	96
Ukraine	29	Italy	48	India	68	Nigeria	95
Poland	22	France	43	Germany	62	DR Congo	91
Spain	19	Philippines	34	Nigeria	61	Russia	85
Brazil	17	Spain	33	DR Congo	53	Ethiopia	67

We notice here that in 1900 eight of the top ten countries as far as church membership is concerned were European: Eastern European countries such as Russia, Ukraine and Poland, and Western European countries such as Germany, France, Britain, Italy and Spain. The only non-European countries were the USA as number one and Brazil as number ten. In 1970 the USA was still at the top and Brazil has climbed up to the second position. Of the eight remaining ones there are still six European countries, but Mexico and the Philippines have now joined the list. Then in 2005 there are only two European countries left on the list, Russia and Germany, as Britain, Italy, France, and Spain have been replaced by China, India, Nigeria and DR Congo. And if we again look into the future, we see that in 2025 Russia is the only remaining European country still to be found on the list, as Ethiopia then will have replaced Germany. It is an irony of fate, I would say, that a century after the Russian revolution, Russia is the only European country to survive in the list of top ten countries with high figures of church membership. And likewise, a couple of centuries after the mission revivals swept over the western parts of Europe, these countries are experiencing a global marginalisation as far as church membership is concerned.

INSTITUTIONAL ASPECTS

The details of the two tables presented above can obviously be questioned, but hardly the major trends they reflect. It is an unquestionable fact that Christianity throughout the last century or so has changed from being a typically northern or western religion to becoming a religion of the Global South. And the question to be raised in the present seminar is, then, what consequences this has—and will have—for academic studies of the Old Testament. I will outline some institutional consequences and the rest of the papers in this seminar will point out other consequences.

The institutional consequences are many. All over the world—not only in Europe and North America—the Old Testament is now being studied in universities and theological seminaries. In Brazil, as a major South American example, several institutions offer Master's programmes in Old Testament studies, and both the Methodist University in Sao Paulo and the Ecumenical Theological Faculty in Buenos Aires offer doctoral programmes. In Nigeria, as a major African example, the situation is the same, with a number of institutions offering Master's programmes in Old Testament studies and a few also offering doctoral programmes, such as the University of Nigeria, the University of Ibadan and the University of Ilorin. In India, as a major Asian example, Master's programmes in Old Testament studies are offered in several places, and doctoral programmes are offered by the United Theological College in Bangalore, the Federated Faculty in Kerela and Gurukul Lutheran Theological College in Chennai.

Likewise, all over the world—not only in Europe and North America—there is a multitude of academic organisations, conferences and journals for biblical and Old Testament studies, both on national and regional levels. In Brazil the Network for Popular Reading of the Bible publishes *Revista de Interperetación Biblica Latinoamericana*, but there are also other journals, like *Revista Biblica Brasileira*. In Nigeria the Nigerian Association for Biblical Studies publishes *African Journal of Biblical Studies, Hokma House*; the Centre for Biblical Research publishes *Sapientia Logos*, and articles of biblical studies are also found in more general academic journals like *Orita*. In India there is the Indian Society of Biblical Studies and specialised journals such as *Bible Bhashyam* as well as more general theological journals occasionally including articles in biblical studies, such as *Indian Theological Studies* and *Jeevadhara*.

I would like to use the situation of Old Testament studies in sub-Saharan Africa as a case to illustrate the institutional consequences of Christianity becoming a religion of the Global South. And I will approach the institutional situation in sub-Saharan Africa from two perspectives: first, the establishment of universities and theological seminaries creates the frameworks for Old Testament and biblical studies, and then the establishment of professional organisations and journals creates the frameworks for scholarly interaction and research dissemination in Old Testament or biblical studies.[4]

The first perspective is the establishing of academic institutions with frameworks for Old Testament studies. In 1960, at the dawn of independence, sub-Saharan Africa had six universities and a few dozen theological seminaries, and one could hardly talk about academic Old Testament studies in any of these.[5] At present, half a century later, Africa has around two hundred universities and several hundred theological seminaries, while programmes for graduate and postgraduate Old Testament studies are found in an increasing number of these institutions. The development of such programmes requires senior staff members with doctorates and so from the 1960s one can observe an increasing focus on doctoral training. The following table surveys the number of completed doctoral projects in Old Testament studies, according to the home country of the candidate and decade by decade.[6]

---

[4] See K. Holter, "Old Testament scholarship in Sub-Saharan Africa," in *The Bible in Africa* (eds. G. O. West and M. W. Dube; Leiden: Brill, 2000), 569–581.

[5] See *idem*, *Old Testament Research for Africa: A Critical Analysis and Annotated Bibliography of African Old Testament Dissertations, 1967–2000* (New York: Peter Lang, 2002), 61–86.

[6] *Ibid.*, 65.

	1960s	1970s	1980s	1990s	Total
Burkina Faso			1		1
Burundi			1		1
Cameroon	1		3		4
Centr Afr Rep				1	1
Chad			1	1	2
Dem Rep Congo		1	2	5	8
Eritrea		1		1	2
Gabon			1		1
Ghana			3	1	4
Ivory Coast				1	1
Kenya			1	3	4
Madagascar			1	2	3
Malawi				3	3
Namibia				1	1
Nigeria	1	8	10	15	34
Rwanda	1			2	3
Sierra Leone				1	1
Tanzania		1	1	2	4
Togo		1			1
Uganda			1		1
Zambia				1	1
Zimbabwe		1	1	2	4
Unknown			1	1	2
Total	3	13	28	43	87

Two points should be made here. First, we notice the rapid growth in number, from three doctoral theses in Old Testament studies in the 1960s to thirteen in the 1970s, twenty-eight in the 1980s and forty-three in the 1990s. This growth reflects the establishing of graduate and postgraduate Old Testament programmes in the home contexts of the doctoral candidates. Second, we also notice the strong presence of Nigerian candidates; forty percent of the doctoral candidates are Nigerians. This high percentage reflects the particular Nigerian situation: a combination of a university policy encouraging religious and biblical studies, and a large number of churches that have established their own theological institutions.

The second perspective is the establishment of professional organisations and journals that create the frameworks for continued—post-doctoral—scholarly interaction and research dissemination in Old Testament or biblical studies. The first organisations with a clear focus on biblical studies came into being in the early 1980s. A major example covering the African continent as a whole is the Pan-African Association for Catholic Exegetes (PACE), which was established to promote biblical scholarship within the Roman Catholic Church in Africa. PACE operates through biennial conferences and publication of conference papers in its series of *Proceedings*.[7] Another major example, this one a non-denominational organisation working on a national level, is the Nigerian Association for Biblical Studies (NABIS), established in the mid-1980s to promote biblical research in Nigeria.[8] NABIS operates through annual conferences and publication of articles in its *African Journal of Biblical Studies*; amidst an ocean of academic journals in sub-Saharan Africa this one has survived for more than twenty years as a voice of biblical interpretation from explicit African perspectives.

The experiences of the pioneer organisations from the 1980s eventually inspired others to establish similar organisations; one example is the Association for Biblical Scholarship in Eastern Africa (ABSEA),[9] another is the Ghana Association of Biblical Exegetes (GABES).[10] In addition to such national and regional organisations, the question of establishing a non-denominational, pan-African organisation has sometimes been discussed. However, for various reasons the project never materialised.[11] Similarly, international organisations like the Society of Biblical Literature (SBL) and the International Organization for the Study of the Old Testament (IOSOT) have been able to attract African Old Testament scholars to their congresses only to a very limited degree. The 2007 congress of IOSOT was the first where a scholar from sub-Saharan Africa—Dr. Mary Jerome Obiorah, Nigeria[12]—had been invited to read a main paper (see, though, previous examples of short papers presented by Africans at IOSOT congresses).[13] More successful as far as international and inter-African

---

[7] See A. Kabasele Mukenge, "Association Panafricaine des Exégètes Catholiques," *BOTSA* 8 (2000), 3–5.

[8] See J. O. Akao, "Nigerian Association for Biblical Studies," *BOTSA* 8 (2000), 5–7.

[9] See V. Zinkuratire, "Association for Biblical Scholarship in Eastern Africa," *BOTSA* 8 (2000), 9–10.

[10] See B. A. Ntreh, "Ghana Association of Biblical Exegetes," *BOTSA* 11 (2001), 21–22.

[11] See K. Holter, "Is there a need for a pan-African and non-denominational organization for biblical scholarship?" *BOTSA* 8 (2000), 10–13.

[12] See M. J. Obiorah, "Perception of God's house in the Psalter: A Study of how the Psalmists understand the temple" (Unpubl. main paper, IOSOT Congress, Ljubljana, 2007).

[13] S. G. A. Onibere, "Old Testament sacrifice in African tradition: A case of scapegoatism," in *'Wünschet Jerusalem Frieden': Collected Communications to the XIIth Congress of the International Organisation for the Study of the Old Testament, Jerusalem 1986. Beiträge zur Erforschung des Alten Testaments und des Antiken Judentums* 13 (eds. M. Augustin and K.-D. Schunk; Frankfurt a.M., 1988), 193–203; A. O. Mojola, "Understanding ancient Israelite social structures: Some conceptual confusions" (Unpubl. short paper, IOSOT Congress, Cambridge, 1995); *idem*, "The Chagga scapegoat purification ritual and another re-reading of the goat of *Azazel* in Leviticus 16," *Melita Theologica* 50 (1999), 57—83; D. T. Adamo, "The trends of Old Testament scholarship in Africa" (Unpubl.

collaboration is concerned is actually the Old Testament Society of South Africa (OTSSA),[14] which attracts an increasing number of Africans from north of the river Limpopo to its annual congress, and in whose journal—*Old Testament Essays*—one finds an increasing number of articles from fellow African scholars.

SOUTHERN VS. NORTHERN BIBLICAL HERMENEUTICS

The interaction—or rather, the lack of interaction—between southern (*in casu* sub-Saharan African) and northern (*in casu* European) biblical or Old Testament studies deserves particular attention in a seminar on global biblical hermeneutics, and I would like to address it from two perspectives: the dependence of sub-Saharan African Old Testament studies upon northern research contexts, and the conscious, contextual concerns of the southern guilds.

First, it should not come as a surprise that the vast majority of today's Old Testament researchers in sub-Saharan Africa did their training in northern institutions. The following table presents the relationship between where the scholars of the first generation of sub-Saharan African Old Testament come from (the vertical axis) and where they did their doctoral studies (horizontal axis).[15]

---

short paper, IOSOT Congress, Basel, 2001); A. Kabasele Mukenge, "Lire la Bible dans le contexte africain: approche et perspectives" in *Congress Volume Leiden 2004* (ed. A. Lamaire; Leiden: Brill, 2006), 441–448.

[14] See H. F. van Rooy, "The Old Testament Society of South Africa," *BOTSA* 8 (2000), 7–8.

[15] See Holter, *Old Testament Research for Africa*, 68–75.

GLOBAL HERMENEUTICS?

	Belgium	Cameroon	France	Germany	Italy	Ivory Coast	Kenya	Netherlands	Nigeria	South Africa	Sweden	Switzerland	UK	United States	Total
Burkina Faso					1										1
Burundi		1													1
Cameroon			4												4
Central Afr Rep								1							1
Chad					1									1	2
Dem Rep Congo	4		1		3										8
Eritrea														2	2
Gabon			1												1
Ghana				1	1									2	4
Ivory Coast						1									1
Kenya							1							3	4
Madagascar			3												3
Malawi										2			1		3
Namibia										1					1
Nigeria	1			2	11				10				3	7	34
Rwanda		1			1							1			3
Sierra Leone														1	1
Tanzania					2						1			1	4
Togo					1										1
Uganda													1		1
Zambia										1					1
Zimbabwe													1	3	4
Unknown					2										2
Total	5	1	9	4	23	1	1	1	10	4	1	1	6	20	87

We notice that most of the doctoral theses—around eighty-five percent—are written in Western contexts, and further, that the relationship between the nationality of the researcher and the geographical location of the degree-giving institution in most cases follows old and well-established connections. Research is very much a question of funding, and funding agencies for this kind of research are often located in political or ecclesiastical structures. As for the political level, structures from the colonial past are still reflected, as various forms of political and economic agreements on culture, education and research cooperation tend to bind former colonisers and colonies together. In the present instance this explains, to some extent, why students from Cameroon and Madagascar tend to do their research in France, or why students from the Democratic Republic of the Congo tend to do their research in Belgium. Still, neo-colonial developments are also reflected in the data, such as a sudden American dominance in the 1990s.

At the ecclesiastical level a corresponding pattern can be observed: Roman Catholics tend to get their training in Roman Catholic contexts, especially in pontifical institutions in Rome, and scholars from various Protestant denominations tend to get their training in Protestant institutions in Europe and the USA. As an example, one could say that it is typical that two out of four doctoral candidates from Tanzania, both being Lutherans, did their research in Lutheran institutions in Scandinavia and the USA, whereas the two others, both being Roman Catholics, did their research in pontifical institutions in Rome.

The fact that the funding and institutional location of the doctoral research often follows old and well-established political and ecclesiastical structures may have positive consequences. Many research projects grow out of long-standing networks between Western and African institutional partnerships, and as such they are not isolated cases of research training but a part of more extensive plans for staff building and institutional development. However, there may be negative consequences too. Such old and well-established structures tend to preserve a status quo of various types of imbalance between the two partners. In most cases the Western partner is in control of the financial as well as the (Western) academic networks, and it may regard the African partner as a "daughter" rather than a "sister".

The second perspective on the interaction—or lack of interaction—between southern and northern Old Testament studies concerns the conscious, contextual concerns of the southern guilds. In spite of the heavy dependence upon northern research contexts in their academic training, the members of the southern guilds show a much stronger attention to questions of the contextual, contemporary relevance of Old Testament studies than they were exposed to during their training in the north.

One example is the Pan-African Association of Catholic Exegetes, which explicitly aims to "promote and undertake studies in exegesis which is necessary for the incarnation of the Bible message in local churches within Africa and Madagascar".[16] Another example is the Nigerian Association for Biblical Studies, which states that it aims at "relating biblical interpretation to the life situation in Africa and African societal problems".[17] And a third—and non-African example this time—is the newly established (2006) Society of Asian Biblical Studies (SABS), which aims to "facilitate a broad and open discussion from a variety of

---

[16] See BICAM s.a., "The origin and history of the Catholic Biblical Center for Africa and Madagascar (BICAM)" (http://www.sceam-secam.org/showpdfs.php?id=4, accessed 2009-02-06).

[17] See NABIS s.a., "Nigerian Association for Biblical Studies: History and Aim" (http://www.nabis.8m.com/, accessed 2009-02-06).

perspectives, particularly that of the minorities and marginalised in Asia", and also to "encourage study and interpretation of biblical literature and related literature using traditional and diverse methods and approaches in the varied Asian cultural and lingual contexts".[18]

Conclusion

This contribution has tried to draw some lines in the geographical and institutional structures of a new and global Old Testament studies. The papers following in this volume will fill these structures with flesh and blood, as more examples and more reflection in relation to what it means to interpret the Old Testament in today's global world will be presented.

---

[18] See SABS s.a., "Society of Asian Biblical Studies" (http://www.theology.auckland.ac.nz/uoa/fms/ default/theology/news-and-events/docs/postgraduate/no_28_feb_07.pdf, accessed 2007–06–29), 4.

Part II

CASE STUDIES

Hermeneutical Perspectives on Violence against Women and on Divine Violence in German-Speaking Old Testament Exegesis

GERLINDE BAUMANN

INTRODUCTION

The hermeneutical debate in German-speaking Old Testament exegesis will be illustrated in this article with the help of two examples. The issue of violence against women in the Old Testament is more specific and will be addressed briefly. The matter of divine aggression or violence is broader and receives more detailed analysis, as the topic allows for developing a deeper insight into hermeneutic reflection in general.

VIOLENCE AGAINST WOMEN IN OLD TESTAMENT TEXTS

The first example illustrates briefly the topic of *violence against women in Old Testament texts*. The scene for the German interpretations is set by the debate on domestic violence in society in general. In mainstream exegesis we hardly find any reactions or responses to this issue; it is mostly feminist exegetes who work on this topic. These exegetes draw extensively from the Anglo-American feminist exegetical debates and also from the methods of literary criticism; they adapt contextual hermeneutics and synchronic methodology. The debate focuses on two issues. On the one hand, a number of Old Testament texts about violence against women are criticised (e.g. Gen 19; Judg 19; 2 Sam 13) because of their patriarchal point of view.[1] The texts do not seem to include the views and perspectives of

---

[1] See e.g. E. Seifert, "Lot und seine Töchter. Eine Hermeneutik des Verdachts," in *Feministische Hermeneutik und Erstes Testament. Analysen und Interpretationen* (eds. H. Jahnow *et al.*; Stuttgart: Kohlhammer, 1994), 48–66; I. Müllner, "Tödliche Differenzen. Sexuelle Gewalt als Gewalt gegen andere in Ri 19," in *Von der Wurzel getragen. Christlich-feministische Exegese in Auseinandersetzung mit Antijudaismus* (ed. L. Schottroff and M.-Th. Wacker; BibIS 17; Leiden: Brill, 1996), 81–100; idem, *Gewalt im Hause Davids: Die Erzählung von Tamar und Amnon (2 Sam 13,1–22)*, (HBS 13; Freiburg: Herder, 1997); E. Seifert, *Tochter und Vater im Alten Testament. Eine ideologiekritische Untersuchung zur Verfügungsgewalt von Vätern über ihre Töchter* (Neukirchen-Vluyn: Neukirchener, 1997); U. Bail, *Gegen das Schweigen klagen. Eine intertextuelle Studie zu den Klagepsalmen Ps 6 und Ps 55 und der Erzählung von der Vergewaltigung Tamars* (Gütersloh: Gütersloher

women. On the other hand, the prophetic texts about divine violence against metaphorical "women" (such as Israel or Jerusalem) are analysed and criticised (e.g. Isa 47; Jer 2:13; Ezek 16:23; Hos 1–3; Nah 3:4–7).[2] An important point of critique is that these texts have the potential to legitimate or stimulate human (male) violence against women: if God's violence against *his* women is justified, why not human (male) violence against *his* wife or women?

One hermeneutical strategy to cope with these texts is to use diachronic historical-critical methods to distinguish between the text and its redaction; the latter is found to be more patriarchal than the original text.[3] Another strategy lies in looking for "counter-texts". This way, in some texts one can find inner-biblical voices of critique against such form of violence.[4] A third strategy is to look for women's or female voices in the texts.[5] In following this line some exegetes outline a hermeneutics which tries to read the texts of violence against women as texts which are based on the experience of victims.[6] A more creative approach reads lament psalms as the words of victims of domestic violence. In this intertextual perspective the reader gives words to the silenced woman Tamar (2 Sam 13).[7] In such intertextual, synchronic and literary readings we find the position that texts about (any kind of) violence can be read as documents of victims who struggle with what they have experienced. Biblical texts on any kind of violence serve as possible means to cope with violence—in biblical times as well as in our time.

Verlagshaus, 1998); R. Jost, *Gender, Sexualität und Macht in der Anthropologie des Richterbuches* (BWANT 9; Stuttgart: Kohlhammer, 2006).

[2] See e.g. C. Maier, "Jerusalem als Ehebrecherin in Ezechiel 16. Zur Verwendung und Funktion einer biblischen Metapher," in *Feministische Hermeneutik und Erstes Testament. Analysen und Interpretationen* (eds. H. Jahnow *et al.*; Stuttgart: Kohlhammer, 1994), 85–105; M.-Th. Wacker, "Figurationen des Weiblichen im Hosea-Buch" (HBS 8; Freiburg: Herder, 1996); G. Baumann, "Liebe und Gewalt. Die Ehe als Metapher für das Verhältnis JHWH-Israel in den Prophetenbüchern" (SBS 185; Stuttgart: Kohlhammer, 2000); translated version: G. Baumann, "Love and Violence. The Imagery of Marriage for YHWH and Israel in the Prophetic Books" (trans. L.M. Maloney; Collegeville: Liturgical Press, 2003); M. Häusl, "Bilder der Not. Weiblichkeits- und Geschlechtermetaphorik im Buch Jeremia" (HBS 37; Freiburg: Herder, 2003).

[3] This line is followed by e.g. Maier, "Jerusalem" and Wacker, "Figurationen".

[4] See e.g. Baumann, "Liebe und Gewalt" / "Love and Violence".

[5] This approach was developed by F. van Dijk-Hemmes and A. Brenner, *On Gendering Texts. Female and Male Voices in the Hebrew Bible* (BibIS 1; Leiden: Brill, 1993).

[6] See I. Müllner, "Gegen ihren Willen. Sexuelle Gewalt im Alten Testament," *Essener Unikate* 21 (2003), 8–21.

[7] See Bail, *Gegen das Schweigen*.

DIVINE VIOLENCE

Divine violence has been discussed in Germany since the late 1970s.[8] This debate was initially related to the peace movement. More recently the question of YHWH as perpetrator or aggressor became a relevant research topic in German exegesis in the debate on monotheism and its possibly negative consequences. The ways of interpreting images of God as perpetrator in the Old Testament are quite heterogeneous. The scheme below tries to systematise the main strategies in twelve points.[9]

The first strategy (I) lies in *skipping* the problem by not interpreting the texts or just overlooking the problem. As an implicit hermeneutics, this strategy is widespread: there are only very few articles on "violence" or "God and violence" in monographs on Old Testament theology[10] or in reference works.[11] Reasons for this strategy may be that the starting point for theology in Germany is not often seen in problems of 'ordinary life' such as violence, but in the first place as deriving from scholarly, academic questions.

Close to the first hermeneutical strategy is (II) one which *leaves out* the problem of violence in the image of God. In some Old Testament theologies[12] this is caused by the structure of the approach: if theology focuses only on *one* aspect of God—in most cases 'love'—then it is difficult to integrate the violent or other not-loving aspects of God. An alternative could be to create a concept of theology

---

[8] Review of literature on the topic in: J. Ebach, *Das Erbe der Gewalt. Eine biblische Realität und ihre Wirkungsgeschichte* (Gütersloh: Gütersloher Verlagshaus, 1980); N. Lohfink (ed.), *Gewalt und Gewaltlosigkeit im Alten Testament* (QD 96; Freiburg: Herder, 1983), esp. 15–50 and 225–247. For the topic of divine aggression or violence in German exegesis see G. Baumann, *Gottesbilder der Gewalt im Alten Testament verstehen* (Darmstadt: Wissenschaftliche Buchgesellschaft, 2006) with coordinates for a hermeneutic of divine violence in the Old Testament (15–36), an analysis of German scholarly literature since 1970 (37–72), a systematisation of the approaches (72–79), the outline of a new approach (79–83), and five interpretations of biblical texts which cover different aspects of divine violence (Josh 10:10; Ps 74:13–17; Ezek 23; Nah 1:2–8; and Job).

[9] See a more elaborate version of this scheme in *idem, Gottesbilder der Gewalt*, 72–79.

[10] See N. Lohfink, "Altes Testament—die Entlarvung der Gewalt," in *Weltgestaltung und Gewaltlosigkeit. Ethische Aspekte des Alten und Neuen Testaments in ihrer Einheit und ihrem Gegensatz* (ed. N. Lohfink and R. Pesch; Düsseldorf: Patmos, 1978), 49; idem, "'Gewalt' als Thema alttestamentlicher Forschung," in *Gewalt und Gewaltlosigkeit im Alten Testament* (ed. N. Lohfink; QD 96; Freiburg: Herder, 1983), 15–50 (p. 17).

[11] This is also seen by A. Michel, "Gott und Gewalt gegen Kinder im Alten Testament" (FAT 37; Tübingen: Mohr-Siebeck, 2003), 2–3.

[12] See e.g.: H. D. Preuss, *Theologie des Alten Testaments. 1. JHWHs erwählendes und verpflichtendes Handeln* (Stuttgart: Kohlhammer, 1991); idem, *Theologie des Alten Testaments. 2. Israels Weg mit JHWH* (Stuttgart: Kohlhammer, 1992); O. Kaiser, *Der Gott des Alten Testaments. Wesen und Wirken. Theologie des Alten Testaments Teil 2. Jahwe, der Gott Israels, Schöpfer der Welt und des Menschen* (Göttingen: Vandenhoeck, 1998).

which integrates a certain tension into the image of God, such as Walter Brueggemann's.[13]

A third (III) strategy *justifies* divine violence. Approaches which use this strategy choose a view which is very positive towards the justification of the divine violence which we find, for example, in Deuteronomistic theology or in many prophetic books: Israel or Jerusalem has sinned and therefore God punishes the people. Some authors see a kind of divine pedagogy in God's reprimanding of his people, which in the end leads to a positive result.

The problem of God's violence in the Old Testament can be seen from a different perspective (IV) as being *overcome*[14] by the New Testament's God of love and by Jesus of Nazareth being the Christ.[15] In using this strategy one leaves the problem of divine violence in the Old Testament to Judaism—and it favours anti-Judaism as it is only the "God of the Jews" who is inclined to violence. Another weak point of this strategy is that it overlooks a lot of New Testament texts in which we find violent images of God and Jesus.[16] The problem of divine violence is also evident in the New Testament and not solved in it.

Sometimes as part of the fourth strategy an *evolutionary scheme* (V) can be found in the development of the image of God in the Bible: divine violence

---

[13] W. Brueggemann, *Theology of the Old Testament. Testimony, Dispute, Advocacy* (Minneapolis, Minn.: Fortress, 1997). Brueggemann does evaluate and to a certain extent also positively estimate violent images of God as "counter-testimony" to the "core testimony" of the loving God.

[14] According to Michel (*Gott und Gewalt*, 4), this strategy could also be called substitutional ("Substitutionstheologie"); it is tied to a certain hermeneutics in which the Old Testament is seen to be superseded by the New.

[15] Such a strategy can be found in the approaches of H. D. Preuss, "Alttestamentliche Aspekte zu Macht und Gewalt," in *Macht und Gewalt. Leitlinien lutherischer Theologie zur politischen Ethik heute. Erarbeitet von einem theologischen Ausschuß im Auftrag des Landeskirchenrates der Evangelisch-Lutherischen Kirche in Bayern* (ed. H. Greifenstein; Hamburg: Lutherisches Verlagshaus, 1978), 113–134; or partly in: W. Gross and K.-J. Kuschel, *"Ich schaffe Finsternis und Unheil!" Ist Gott verantwortlich für das Übel?* (Mainz: Matthias Grünewald, 1992), 211–213.

[16] Texts can be found in: J. Ebach, "Der Gott des Alten Testaments—ein Gott der Rache? Versuch einer Klärung einer gerade von Christen immer wieder gestellten Frage," *JK* 55 (1994), 130–139; K. Berger, *Wie kann Gott Leid und Katastrophen zulassen?* (Stuttgart: Kohlhammer, 1996); *idem*, "Der 'brutale Jesus.' Gewaltsames Wirken und Verkündigung Jesu," *BiKi* 51 (1996), 119–127; H. Ritt, "Rachephantasie, infantiles Weltbild, psychischer Konflikt? Gewalt in der Offenbarung des Johannes," *BiKi* 51 (1996), 128–132; V. A. Lehnert, "Wenn der liebe Gott 'böse' wird—Überlegungen zum Zorn Gottes im Neuen Testament," *ZNT* 9 (2002), 15–25; or M. Leutzsch, "Gewalt und Gewalterfahrung im Neuen Testament. Ein vergessenes Thema der neutestamentlichen Wissenschaft?" *ZNT* 17 (2006), 2–13.

becomes less—and less severe—in the process described in the Bible.[17] In the early history of Israel God uses violence (e.g. in the "Holy War"); then there are more traces of inner-biblical criticism of divine violence (e.g. in the Servant of the Lord in Dt-Isa), until divine violence reaches its end in Jesus being crucified. This strategy is also in danger of favouring anti-Judaism.

The theory of the cultural anthropologist René Girard[18] is well known mainly in the Catholic discussion on divine violence. In Girard's concept (VI) it seems possible to put an end to all forms of violence by making a *sacrifice*—which in the Christian context is Jesus of Nazareth. This is, of course, another interpretation of the Old Testament from the New Testament perspective and therefore bears the same problems already mentioned above (IV). Another critical point is, then, that in Girard's scheme violence is looked at without recognising the historical context of biblical texts.[19] Cultural differences between ancient Israel and today's societies are not relevant in this model. Sociological and anthropological research has shown, however, that violence is closely linked to specific sociological conditions and problems. This raises doubt whether there can be a general approach—like Girard's—to *all* forms of violence.

A number of scholars are able to look positively at Old Testament texts of violence and divine violence. In this view (VII) the texts *mirror* historical violence present in all ancient Near Eastern societies, including ancient Israel.[20] Old

---

[17] E.g. Lohfink in one of his earlier works (*Weltgestaltung und Gewaltlosigkeit*); see Michel's critique (*Gott und Gewalt*, 2, note 10): "1. Dass die Problembeschreibung so stark auf die sozial- und tiefenpsychologischen Ansätze Girards rekurriert, begrenzt mit Sicherheit die mögliche interpretative Kraft von Lohfinks Beobachtungen und Hypothesen. 2. Die Verschlingung der Gewaltproblematik in die Perspektive einer erlebbaren, aber religionssoziologisch recht enggefaßten Gewaltlosigkeitsutopie hinein ... schwächt ab, was zuvor stark gemacht wurde. 3. Die hermeneutische Vorordnung des NT vor das AT in Sachen 'Gewalt' ... reduziert das AT im wesentlichen eben doch, allen gegenteiligen Beteuerungen zum Trotz, auf einen Anweg der 'Entlarvung der Gewalt' ...."

[18] E.g. R. Girard, *Violence and the Sacred* (trans. P. Gregory; Baltimore: Johns Hopkins University Press, 1977 [Paris 1972]); for the German reception see e.g. R. Schwager, *Brauchen wir einen Sündenbock? Gewalt und Erlösung in den biblischen Schriften* (München: Kösel, 1978).

[19] For more critical points see U. Rüterswörden, "Das Ende der Gewalt? Zu René Girards Buch," in *Der eine Gott der beiden Testamente* (eds. I. Baldermann *et al.*; JBTh 2. Neukirchen-Vluyn: Neukirchener, 1987), 247–256.

[20] This position can be found in a number of approaches: Lohfink, *Weltgestaltung und Gewaltlosigkeit*, 49–53; W. H. Schmidt, "Gott und das Böse. Hinweise auf das Alte Testament," *EvTh* 52 (1992), 7–22 (p. 21); E. Zenger, *Ein Gott der Rache? Feindpsalmen verstehen* (Freiburg: Herder, 1994), 162, 165; M. Görg, *Der un-heile Gott. Die Bibel im Bann der Gewalt* (Düsseldorf: Patmos, 1995), 25; S. Krahe, *Ermordete Kinder und andere Geschichten von Gottes Unmoral* (Würzburg: Echter, 1999), 9, 120; and—partly—O. Fuchs, "Macht und Gewalt in biblischen Texten. Eine praktisch-theologische Auseinandersetzung

Testament texts are not euphemistic about Israelite society and they do not gloss over violence—but they allow the biblical writers to criticise violence. A more psychological approach appreciates the texts because they confront us as individual beings and as communities with our own potential for violence. In this perspective the Old Testament texts can be used to question and criticise present-day readers and their violence.

Close to this view comes the hermeneutics of *remembrance* (VIII), although it takes a more critical stance towards Old Testament texts. This hermeneutics has been developed in feminist exegesis. It is based on the theory that texts about violence mirror violence which actually happened historically. An example: the rape of women in the context of war is seen as a historical image for the metaphor of YHWH as husband who violates and rapes "his" wife Israel/Jerusalem. This metaphor is widely used in the prophetic literature (see above, "Violence against women in Old Testament texts"). The hermeneutics of remembrance tries in its extreme forms to read the texts non-metaphorically, which means that the important part of the text is not the metaphor, but the remembering of the victims of violence *beyond* the metaphor.[21]

A significant number of German-speaking scholars interpret violent images of God in a *historical perspective* (IX). This approach tries to establish a contrast between the texts and their historical or religious-historical background.[22] Seen in this perspective, some of the texts seem to be *fictional* texts. An example: texts in the book of Joshua or in Deuteronomy about the conquest of the land can be called *pure fiction*. Even though this might be true, many scholars think this is enough to explain or to lessen the problematic aspects of the texts. The theological problem of the text is, however, not solved. It only reappears on a different level: now we have to ask *why* these texts were *invented*. Most of the historical approaches do not provide an answer to this question.[23]

Seen from an *ethical or moral perspective* (X), most of the texts about divine violence cause severe problems.[24] Especially in Christian theology, God often functions as an example of morality for believers. One basis of such thinking is the

---

mit dem 'gewalttätigen' Gott der Bibel," in *Praktische Hermeneutik der Heiligen Schrift* (ed. O. Fuchs; PTHe 57; Stuttgart: Kohlhammer, 2004), 438–461.

[21] See Baumann, "Liebe und Gewalt" / "Love and Violence"; Müllner, "Gegen ihren Willen".

[22] This position is—at least in parts—taken by Gross and Kuschel, *Finsternis und Unheil*; E. Otto, *Krieg und Frieden in der hebräischen Bibel und im Alten Orient. Aspekte für eine Friedensordnung in der Moderne* (Stuttgart: Kohlhammer, 1999); A. Schart, "Zwischen Gottes-Krieg und Feindesliebe. Krieg und Frieden in der Bibel," *Essener Unikate* 21 (2003), 62–71, 64–67.

[23] Some of the propositions of W. Dietrich and C. Link, *Die dunklen Seiten Gottes. 1: Willkür und Gewalt.* (Neukirchen-Vluyn: Neukirchener, 1995), and *2: Allmacht und Ohnmacht.* (Neukirchen-Vluyn: Neukirchener, 2000), tend towards this direction.

[24] An example of this position is Krahe, *Ermordete Kinder*.

concept of *imitatio Christi*: believers should in their own lives follow the example of Jesus Christ. This concept is sometimes transferred to the first person of the trinity, which creates the above-mentioned problems. In a political or spiritual situation which tries to legitimise moral values with the help of divine morality, violent images of God are perceived as a great challenge.

Some exegetes try to explain divine violence in the Old Testament by the thought that *God is radically different* from humans and human standards do not apply (XI).[25] God is not a person or a being like humans. The biblical image of God appears to be Janus-faced or miraculous and therefore not fully understandable to us as humans. Often we find dogmatic premises behind such theories, which the authors do not always seem to be aware of. In any case, this position takes into account that God has different aspects or sides. Therefore God is not limited to one aspect as in one of the above-mentioned perspectives (II).

Last but not least, some authors take into consideration the revising or re-working of violent images of God by biblical authors or redactors.[26] These exegetes sometimes look for *counter-texts* or *counter-voices* in the same biblical book or in other biblical books (XII). In a significant number of texts one can find these voices; sometimes the *problematic* texts are semantically linked to the *counter-text*. Other scholars mention inner-biblical critique against violence in a more general way.[27] A problematic aspect of this approach lies in attempting to neutralise the texts about divine violence. This would mean avoiding the problematic texts instead of dealing with them.

This list of hermeneutic positions shows a significant plurality of approaches towards divine violence in the Old Testament in German-speaking scholarship. This is different from the topic of violence against women, mentioned above as the first example. Most of these scholars, however, do not explain their hermeneutics or position themselves in the field of hermeneutics.

My own position tries to form a synthesis of the most productive approaches.[28] A historical hermeneutics, synchronic approaches, and a non-monistic view on the image of God is desirable: historical hermeneutics in general allows us to take into account the differences between the ancient Near Eastern and ancient Israelite world, which are significant in the field of studies of violence. Synchronic or

---

[25] So e.g. Görg, *Der un-heile Gott*, 175; or Krahe, *Ermordete Kinder*, 145–151.

[26] See Zenger, *Ein Gott der Rache?*; R. Scoralick, "Hallelujah für einen gewalttätigen Gott? Zur Theologie von Psalm 135 und 136," *BZ* 46 (2002), 253–272; idem, "Gottes Güte und Gottes Zorn. Die Gottesprädikationen in Ex 34,6f. und ihre intertextuellen Beziehungen zum Zwölfprophetenbuch" (HBS 33; Freiburg: Herder, 2002); or Baumann, "Liebe und Gewalt" / "Love and Violence".

[27] So, Ebach, *Das Erbe der Gewalt*, 30–42; or Walter Dietrich and Moisés Mayordomo, *Gewalt und Gewaltüberwindung in der Bibel* (Zürich: Theologischer Verlag Zürich, 2005).

[28] A more elaborate version in: Baumann, *Gottesbilder der Gewalt*, 79–83.

canonical approaches make it easier to look for counter-voices or counter-texts. A multifaceted view of the image of God avoids the dangers of the strategies (I), (II) and (IV).

CONCLUDING REMARKS

Let me finally add some general remarks on the hermeneutics of German-speaking Old Testament exegesis.

The scholars mentioned in this article represent a minority in German-speaking exegesis. Only a few scholars, especially in Protestant exegesis, work on questions from ordinary life, of which violence is only one, and only a few reflect on hermeneutical questions. Hermeneutics in general is a topic which is not very popular in this sector of scholarship. Many more scholars work on topics derived solely from the academic or scholarly world. Their implicit hermeneutics is one that seeks the historical truth behind the text. This perspective is often combined with a non-contextual perspective that claims neutrality or objectivity.

Aside from this Protestant mainstream just described, there are other positions and alternative hermeneutical approaches that are creative and that adapt canonical, contextual and more synchronic perspectives. In this exegetical branch Anglo-American and other positions from abroad are appreciated and applied productively in German exegesis.

Land in the Old Testament: Hermeneutics from Latin America

ROY H. MAY, JR.

INTRODUCTION

Several years ago I was asked by the United Methodist Church in the USA to write a small study book for church congregations about Joshua and the conquest of the Promised Land. When I discussed Josh 13–19, I entitled the chapter "Land Reform in Canaan" because, I wrote, "land reform would be the first step toward a new way of organising social life." According to verse 13c, Yahweh commanded Joshua to "allot the land to Israel". So I explained that the text showed that "a massive land redistribution program was undertaken to ensure fields for small farmers".[1] One of my pre-publication expert reviewers, a professor of Old Testament at a major university, expressed surprise at my statement, pencilling in the margin of my manuscript, "What's this all about...?"

Land or agrarian reform was foreign to the US-based Old Testament scholar who had never experienced the struggle for land by landless Latin American peasants. Yet in Latin America, whenever I asked students what "allot the land" means, they inevitably and quickly responded "land reform". Indeed, among Latin American scholars who have worked on the Old Testament land themes, "land reform" is prominent in their interpretations. My point, which I will develop in what follows, is that the biblical reader's or scholar's own reality and historical experience influence how biblical themes are studied and interpreted. Reality and experience become a kind of filter through which the Bible is understood.

This can distort the (exegetical) meanings of texts, but it also can provide insights that otherwise would not be had, and certainly opens unforeseen apologetic possibilities. This is the case with land in the Old Testament, where European and US American scholars have long dealt with the theme, but hardly as the struggle for agrarian or land reform or as the utopian vision of landless peasants. Of course we can debate the adequacy of such interpretation-from-experience, but it does provide insightful perspectives on the land in the Old Testament and clearly brings these old texts alive for contemporary poor farmers. Before proceeding, it will be useful to describe briefly biblical hermeneutics as they have emerged in Latin America.[2]

---

[1] R. H. May, *Joshua and the Promised Land*. (New York: Women's Division of the General Board of Global Ministries of the United Methodist Church, 1997), 29.

[2] My discussion will be based on literature in Spanish and Portuguese; all translations are mine. For an English language presentation of hermeneutics and Bible study in Latin

BIBLICAL HERMENEUTICS IN LATIN AMERICA

The Brazilian theologian Leonardo Boff argues that "there is a structural isoformism of situations between the time of Jesus [that is, biblical times], and our own: objective oppression and dependence subjectively lived as contrary to God's designs".[3] Suggesting such a parallelism between biblical reality and contemporary Latin American reality has an important methodological role in biblical hermeneutics in Latin America. The parallelism, however, is not necessarily literal, but rather entails a "creative fidelity" between the then of the Bible and the now of today. It is the spirit of the text that makes the Bible relevant and alive today.[4] We look for "core meanings" that are transferred to a new situation and time as the text is re-read and interpreted "from ourselves", that is, on the basis of contemporary reality.[5] We move from our situation to the biblical text and back to our situation. This "hermeneutical circularity"[6] is the key to the text's kerygmatic relevance. Indeed, it is our own situation that enables us to enter into the kerygmatic meaning the text holds, because through it we can "pre-comprehend" what the text is about.[7] Thus the hermeneutical task is to seek "creative fidelity" between the Bible and contemporary reality in order to discover the "core meaning" that makes the text comprehensible today.

Pablo Richard (Chile/Costa Rica) also proffers the central importance of a "historical subject" through whom a text is interpreted: the poor. Richard argues that a "hermeneutic of liberation" means reading the text through the eyes of the poor; in the case of the land, the historical subject is the landless peasant. This enables the text not only to be relevant to the poor, but also to be understood as subversive of contemporary reality.[8] This means that it is different to study the land texts within the academic halls of a First World university than to do so with a group of peasant farmers struggling against a large landowner to acquire small fields of their own. In this sense, Richard argues, "The objective ... isn't fundamentally the Bible itself, but the discernment and communication of the Word of God today in the world of the poor".[9] This requires, Richard continues, a

---

America, consult P. Richard, "Interpreting and Teaching the Bible in Latin America," *Interpretation* 4 (2002), 378–386.

[3] L. Boff, *Jesucristo y liberación del hombre* (Madrid: Ediciones Cristianidad, 1981).

[4] C. Boff, *Teologia e prática. Teologia do político e suas mediaçoes* (Petróplis: Vozes, 1978). [English: *Theology and Praxis. Epistemological Foundation*. Maryknoll, N.Y.: Orbis Books, 1987).]

[5] J. S. Croatto, *Liberación y libertad, Pautas hermenéuticas* (Buenos Aires: Ediciones Nuevo Mundo, 1973), 145.

[6] *Ibid.*

[7] *Ibid.*, 146.

[8] P. Richard, "Lectura popular de la Biblia en América Latina. Hermenéutic de la liberación," *RIBLA* 1 (1988), 30–48.

[9] *Ibid.*, 33.

"hermeneutical rupture" because traditional First World readings have obscured or even eliminated the poor as the text's historical subject; texts have been "expropriated" by the powerful to serve their own interests and must be "re-appropriated" by the poor.[10]

Narciso Farias of Brazil, in a study of the biblical land tradition, states these ideas directly: "When we read the Bible, taking the land as reference, as the promise of Yahweh, the text opens an impressive contact with the events of today's reality ... Upon finding that the Bible is a story of popular struggle, it becomes alive in such a way that it rescues the concrete story of a people in their struggle for life, continually in search of the promised land."[11] Barros and Caravias repeat the idea: "The word 'adamah insists that there is a relation between people and the earth. It refers to the peasant, the simple one, without social value."[12] For these authors and others, the historical subject is the peasant farmer.

Methodologically, then, biblical studies and theological work in general in Latin America typically begin with discussions of contemporary reality. For example, Marcelo Barros (Brazil) and José Luis Caravias (Paraguay) begin their important book on the land, *Teologia da Terra*,[13] with presentations on the land situation. Only in their third chapter do they begin their discussion of the biblical land themes. To follow this methodology, then, I will briefly present the land situation in Latin America.

LAND IN LATIN AMERICA TODAY

With neoliberal economics, "globalisation" and rapid urbanisation, land has virtually disappeared from the public agenda. This is partly because most Latin Americans now live in cities, a fact that often obscures the demographic reality that millions still live in rural areas. Indeed, living in cities is preferable to the rural areas because it is in rural areas that poverty is the most grinding. At least thirty-seven percent of Latin America's poor are rural but in Bolivia, Guatemala, Honduras, Nicaragua, Paraguay and Peru—countries with large indigenous populations—at least half the population is rural and seventy percent of the rural population lives in often extreme poverty. Even in Mexico, a country that has strongly embraced neoliberal economic policies, thirty-one percent of the rural people do not have sufficient income to pay for a minimum food basket.[14] Clearly

---

[10] *Ibid.*, 40–47.

[11] N. Farias, "Libertar a terra, salvar a vida—A libertaçao da terra," *Estudos Bíblicos* 19 (1988), 26–41.

[12] M. Barros and J. L. Caravias, *Teologia de la tierra* (Madrid: Ediciones Paulinas, 1988), 188.

[13] *Ibid.*

[14] World Bank, "Beyond the City: the Rural Contribution to Development." Press release, February 14, 2005.

the root of this rural poverty is landlessness. But today land reform is too often viewed as an atavistic throwback to the "immature" times of revolution and social struggle. Now, it is argued, land tenure is best assured and shaped by markets and modernisation for export. Yet these policies of the last twenty or so years hardly have solved the problem of social injustice and just land tenure; rather they have exacerbated them, often causing severe and violent conflicts. Nevertheless, if the struggle for land reform is muted in comparison to previous years, land continues to be a serious problem for Latin America's peasant farmers and indigenous peoples.[15]

According to the Organisation of American States (OAS):

> Latin America has the greatest inequality in land tenure compared to the other regions of the world. In the 70s and 80s...it was possible to find countries where only 6 percent of the population had control of the land while 94 percent was landless. In the same period at least 85 percent of the countries [showed] 60 percent (at times 70 percent as in Argentina and Brazil) of the population without secure access to land.[16]

Continuing, the OAS explains:

> The pattern of land tenure in Latin America and the Caribbean shows that the majority of the cultivable land is in the hands of a landowning elite and the State as unproductive latifundium [large estates] while peasants and small farmers that practice subsistence agriculture are concentrated in minifundium [micro estates] and marginal land.[17]

Furthermore indigenous people are especially affected because of the forty-three million of them, "approximately ninety percent depend on the land and natural resources for their subsistence." Yet their territories are insecure and often remain undefined legally.

The consequence of such unjust land tenure is evident: "Without access to land and the conditions that permit tenure security, landless peasants and poor rural communities will not have the possibility of bettering their means of subsistence", the OAS correctly explains.[18]

This situation gave rise to the church's concern for land as a justice issue in the 1970s (greatly inspired by the establishment of the Pastoral Land Commission of the Roman Catholic Church in Brazil in 1975 with the purpose "to face the latent

---

[15] M. D. Martins, *El Banco Mundial y la tierra, ofensiva y resisrtencia en América Latina, Afrina y Asia*. (San José: DEI, 2005).

[16] Organization of American States, "Tenencia de la Tierra: Compartiendo información y experiencias para la sostenibilidad". Serie de política 10 (abril 2006). www.oas.org/dsd/policy_series/10_spa.pdf

[17] *Ibid.*

[18] *Ibid.*

and existing conflict between agribusiness and landless farmers..."[19]) and biblical interpretations that both reflect and drive that concern. This same situation continues to shape biblical, theological and pastoral work in Latin America.[20]

LATIN AMERICAN READINGS OF THE OLD TESTAMENT LAND TRADITIONS

Readings of the biblical land themes emphasise three principal points of focus: (1) land as peasant property, vital for subsistence; (2) land as spirituality, vital for one's relationship to God; (3) land as struggle, vital for social justice.

Let me illustrate each of these focal points.

LAND AS PEASANT PROPERTY, VITAL FOR SUBSISTENCE

Studies of the Old Testament land theme place great emphasis on land as cultivable fields and family property necessary for subsistence. Farias explains:

> When we speak of the land the image of peasant farmers struggling for a small field as the condition for survival, appears. Our hope is similar to the patriarchs', to whom the Bible refers. It [the Bible] is the narrative of peasants struggling for land....Yahweh takes sides in social conflict in favour of those afflicted and guarantees them possession of the land: ʾadamah = agricultural land for sustaining life.[21]

As often among peasants, land is not understood as private but communal; the community or family is the owner, not individuals.[22] This too is stressed in Latin America. Again Farias explains:

> When biblical faith affirms that the land pertains only to Yahweh, this means to deny the "right" of property to whoever wants it. No one can claim the "right" to ownership of the land. From the perspective of faith, land as private possession is an abomination, and the land becomes damned. For this the biblical texts (the prophets) accuse without pity landowners—usurpers—and animate the dispossessed.[23]

---

[19] Comissao Pastoral da Terra, *CPT: Pastoral e Compromisso* (Petrópolis: CPT, 1983), 71.

[20] This affirmation refers to those who work within a liberationist perspective; the vast majority of Christians in Latin America are traditional Roman Catholics, Pentecostals or evangelical fundamentalists. These groups do not do hermeneutics as described in this paper.

[21] Farias, "Libertar a terra", 26.

[22] F. Ellis, *Peasant Economics, Farm Households and Agrarian Development.* (Cambridge: Cambridge University Press, 1988).

[23] Farias, "Libertar a terra", 27.

The land is inheritance (*nahalah*), meaning that only Yahweh is the true owner. For this reason, Farias and many others explain, the land was distributed equally and could not be bought or sold. For Latin Americans, the reason for this biblical position is clear: "Thus the land remained family property and preserved equality of distribution. This was a way to protect small farmers against encroachments by the large estates."[24]

Land, then, is above all agricultural property to be worked by peasant farmers.

LAND AS SPIRITUALITY, VITAL FOR ONE'S RELATION TO GOD

Land, however, is always more than agricultural soil. "In the Bible, the land fulfils a fundamental role in the very depth of our existence. The human being comes from the land, lives the land, grows in the land and, returns to the land. In more than one sense, 'the land makes the human' and each one is a son or daughter of the land."[25] Traditions of the life-giving qualities of the earth are common in Latin American indigenous and peasant societies.[26] Land is identity and origin. It connects humans with all life. Places are sacred and are to be respected. José Luis Caravias from Paraguay explains, "Between people and the earth there is an intimate tie." It is "Mother Earth".[27] The biblical ʾerets is interpreted in this sense. "The land—ʾerets ... is a constitutive theme of biblical faith, indeed central to it. It is the place where a people relates to Yahweh, and thus it is the guarantee of hope for life, the place where a people is guaranteed its identity."[28] Also, the idea of land as inheritance not only has implications for its distribution; it signifies an ethic, a whole way of understanding and relating to it. One cannot treat the land or buy and sell it as it suits one. Rather, one is obligated to care for and to use it in ways that are just and respond to the needs of the poor. The land is God's gift and it is sacred.[29]

LAND AS STRUGGLE, VITAL FOR SOCIAL JUSTICE

This focal point has received the most attention in Latin America because—especially between 1960 and 1990, when much of the biblical scholarship on land emerged—many countries enacted agrarian reforms and there were active peasant and revolutionary movements pressuring for land redistribution. George Pixley, working from Latin America, suggested that Israel had its origin in a liberation

---

[24] *Ibid.*, 39.
[25] J. I. Alfaro, "Terra prometida: Sacramento da Libertaçao do Exodo". *Estudos Bíblicos* 13 (1987), 9–20.
[26] Barros and Caravias, *Teologia de la tierra*, 71–126.
[27] J. L. Caravias, "Lutar pela terra," *Estudos Bíblicos* 13 (1987), 37–49.
[28] Farias, "Libertar a terra", 26. See also Caravias, "Lutar pela terra".
[29] Alfaro, "Terra prometida", 12–15.

struggle. "[T]he tribes threw off the yoke of the kings of Canaan when the Spirit of Yahweh took possession of an Israelite who called the people of Israel to struggle for their liberation."[30] Francisco Rubeaux of Brazil affirms that "It was necessary to fight, to go to war in order to occupy the land, and that is what the Israelites did."[31] The establishment of "Israel" was a "peasant solution" to social crisis and oppression.[32] This was because the land was occupied by the kings of Canaan, "little autocrats" who oppressed the peasant people through their control of city states.[33] The "Canaanite system",[34] dominated by the kings and aristocrats, marginalised the common peasants from the land and monopolised economic benefits for the powerful class.[35] The "Hebrews" with their tradition of liberation from Egypt, different from the "Canaanites", believed that the land should be distributed justly among the peasants. The "Hebrews" rebelled against the "Canaanites" in order to transform Canaan into a just, peasant society.[36] Thus Barros and Caravias conclude:

> About land tenancy the difference between Hebrew and Canaanite beliefs is basic. Yahweh had no predelict children who should receive property to the land, excluding the majority. The land was promised and given to all the people equally, without exclusivity or privileges. For this reason Yahweh took sides with those-without-land and struggled with them so that they would get it... The liberation from Egypt is the archetype of the flight from the Canaanite system. The conquest of the land under Joshua can be the archetype for struggles in search of autonomous economic and political existence.[37]

In the literature from Latin America the books of Joshua and Judges are interpreted as relating peasant rebellions against large landowners by smallholder, peasant farmers.[38] Clearly the "peasant rebellion" model developed extensively by Norman Gottwald[39] dominates Latin American biblical scholarship because of its

---

[30] J. Pixley, *Reino de Dios.* (Buenos Aires: La Aurora, 1977). [English: *God's Kingdom. A Guide for Biblical Studies.* Maryknoll, N.Y.: Orbis Books, 1981].

[31] F. Rubeaux, "A lei do hérèm: O campo contra a cidade". *Estudos Bíblicos* 19 (1988), 18–25.

[32] M. Schwantes, "Las tribus de Yavé: Una experiencia paradigmática," in *Quema y siembra. De la conquista espiritual al descubrimiento de una nueva evangelización.* (ed. Paulo Suess; Quito: Abya Yala, 1990), 209–228.

[33] Rubeaux, "A lei do hérèm", 88, and Schwantes, "Las tribus de Yavé".

[34] Barros and Caravias, *Teología de la tierra*, 137–139.

[35] Schwantes, "Las tribus de Yavé", 213.

[36] *Ibid.*, 217.

[37] Barros and Caravias, *Teología de la tierra*, 145–146.

[38] See e.g. C. Dreher, "Josue: ¿modelo de conquistador?" *RIBLA* 12 (1992), 49–67.

[39] N. K. Gottwald, *The Tribes of Yahweh* (Maryknoll, N.Y.: Orbis Books, 1985).

perceived affinity with the Latin American reality.[40] The struggle for land is nothing less than a sacred struggle: it is God's own struggle.[41]

In addition to the conquest of the land stories, the Jubilee (Lev 25) has much importance in Latin America. The themes of liberation and land redistribution are often highlighted. The Jubilee is viewed as a kind of utopian vision of a just society that is to be emulated today.[42] Along the same lines, other texts such as Deut 15, Isa 5:8 or Mic 2:1–5 also draw scholarly and apologetic interest. Bible workshops with peasant farmers have often used these texts to promote biblical knowledge and movements for social justice.[43] The Old Testament land traditions become a kind of allegory that gives divine blessing to today's land struggles.

Conclusion

In these texts Latin Americans find an "isoformism" with the struggles for land today, such as the Brazilian Movement of Landless Labourers (MST), and the Zapatista Revolutionary Movement in Mexico, or movements against large hydroelectric plants (Brazil, Guatemala, Chile), or the struggles of indigenous peoples for legal rights to their ancestral territories (Brazil, Chile, Bolivia). The large landowners and agribusinesses are today's "Canaanites" and the peasants are "Hebrews". Thus these ancient Old Testament stories are interpreted as maintaining "creative fidelity" between the "then" of the text and the "now" of today. Today's social reality is believed to provide insights into the biblical world that allows accurate exegesis. Apologetically, the stories are used to give moral legitimacy to the struggles of peasants and indigenous people for land and just social

---

[40] See e.g. Pixley, *Reino de Dios* and J. Pixley, "La toma de la tierra de Canaán. ¿Libereación o despojo?" *Taller de Teología* 12 (1983), 5–14; Barros and Caravias, *Teología de la tierra*; Farias "Libertar a terra"; J. L. Sierra, "Lucha por la tierra, lucha de Dios," *Christus* 628 (1989), 11–26; C. Mesters, *Un proyecto de Dios. La presencia de Dios entre el pueblo oprimido* (Bogotá: Ediciones Paulinas, 1990); Schwantes, "Las tribus de Yavé"; Dreher, "Josué: ¿modelo de conquistador?", among others.

[41] Sierra, "Lucha por la tierra".

[42] Barros and Caravias, *Teología de la tierra*, 189–190; Programa Común de Biblia, *El campesino lee la Biblia* (Belo Horizonte: Centro de Estudos Bíblicos, 1988).

[43] For a decade beginning in the late 1980s I conducted such workshops in Central America, especially Guatemala. Many of these were organised by social action and indigenous peoples' programmes of the Presbyterian Church. Among the aims of these events were: (1) To create awareness about the importance of analysing the causes of problems related to land and farmers; (2) To understand together in what sense biblical reflection relates to the land. I often began these activities with a study of Naboth (1 Kgs 21) in order to draw attention to the contemporary reality of land-related violence, and then moved to other texts, such as the Jubilee (Lev 25) and the prophets, among others, always with the purpose of supporting peasants in their struggle for justice.

arrangements. Rubeaux states this directly: "To conquer the land is a just re-vindication; to defend your land is a sacred right".[44]

---

[44] Rubeaux, "A lei do hérèm", 25.

Reading the Old Testament from a Nigerian Background: A Woman's Perspective

MARY JEROME OBIORAH

INTRODUCTION

In spite of the fast development being experienced in most sectors of life in Nigeria and an increase in the number of women educated in various walks of life, the situation of women with respect to literacy still needs improvement. This is reflected in different approaches of Nigerian women to the Old Testament. This essay studies Nigerian women's understanding of the Old Testament and their varied responses to it, particularly how their socio-cultural background determines their internalisation of the Sacred Scripture. Sources utilised in this contribution are tripartite: literary works by some women, questionnaires, and personal interactions with women from various Nigerian tribes and Christian communities. Besides stating their ages, Christian denominations, tribes and academic qualifications, the women interviewed were requested to express their personal views on the Old Testament and how the Sacred Texts affect their lives as women. The results of this investigation are presented in five interrelated steps, which form the next five sections of this article:
- Nigerian women readers of the Old Testament;
- Levels of meaning;
- Social background of the readers;
- The readers' social background with respect to the Old Testament;
- The readers' wide-ranging responses.

WOMEN READERS OF THE OLD TESTAMENT

In this context the phrase "women readers of the Old Testament" stands for the extensive groups of women who have access to the Bible and whose levels of literacy and social backgrounds condition their approaches to the Sacred Texts. They are Christian women who belong to different tribes and to numerous Christian communities in the country. One can distinguish at least three large groups of women readers.

There are in the first place those Christian women who, as a result of their limited level of formal education, have access to the texts of the Old Testament only by listening to readings in their religious services. These readings are often in the vernacular, very accessible and understood, and generally it is the male leaders who interpret these biblical texts.

Readers in the second group, whose number is indeed growing every day because of the increase in the number of women who embark on formal education, are literate and more enlightened than those in the first group. Their contact with the Bible is not limited to what they hear in the religious celebrations because many of them possess copies of the Bible in various English versions. Women in this group usually continue their personal study of the Sacred Texts in their homes, in other social groups outside their Church premises and in their own research.[1]

A handful of women who have had the privilege of doing formal theological studies and a limited number who have specialised in biblical studies are in the third group. These are mainly lecturers in the few theological schools and other higher education institutions in the country. Some of them are also leaders in their Christian communities.

LEVELS OF MEANING

The differences in the academic backgrounds of women affect their approaches to the Old Testament and the kind of information they look for in the Bible. In spite of the inherent difficulties in understanding some texts of the Bible, particularly the Old Testament, the majority of women in the first group generally consider the Sacred Scriptures as God's word or God's self-communication. It is sacrosanct and therefore it should be taken as it is presented to us. The stories of the origins of the world and similar texts, for instance, are not questioned. Those who have the right of pulpit and who have to address heterogeneous groups of persons do not normally explore beyond the literal meaning of the biblical texts. Women in the first group of readers mentioned above who are exposed to the sermons they receive from the pulpit, therefore do not go beyond the literal meaning either. Sometimes attempts to lead this group to a deeper sense of the biblical text are met with untold difficulties because they are inadequately prepared for receiving other views on Scripture.

Readers in the second group approach the text not only with faith but also with a critical mind.[2] The few experts answer some of these women's questions with caution. Prudence is necessary, because many of the readers lack the necessary

---

[1] Cf. R. N. Edet, "Christianity and African Women's Rituals," in *The Will to Arise: Women, Tradition and the Church in Africa* (ed. M. A. Oduyoye and M. R. A. Kanyoro; New York: Orbis Books, 1992), 25–39. Edet, a senior lecturer in a Nigerian university, discovers in the Old Testament texts (see page 28 of her article) matrices of some religious practices in Nigeria that militate against women's human rights.

[2] M. A. Oduyoye, "Violence against Women: A Challenge to Christian Theology," *Journal of Inculturation Theology* 1 (1994), 48–50. The author employs the biblical accounts of creation, especially the creation of human beings in God's image, in explaining the equality of both genders.

prerequisites for undertaking real exegetical work. On the other hand, some questions are left unattended to or wrongly interpreted by those who have not done a formal study of the Sacred Scriptures.

Women in the third group of readers have their own distinctive difficulties. Descending to a level far below their academic training is not an easy task. However, they have to do so; otherwise the communication gap will become a trench. A good number of these women read the Scriptures with faith but as one would expect, because they are the most exposed to scientific biblical studies, they are more critical than those in the second group. A comment from one of the women illustrates this point:

> The Hebrew creation myth in Genesis, or rather their male-centred interpretations over the years, similarly displayed a gender bias that has become very deeply embedded in the human psyche. The most detrimental of such misogynist myths that derive from a literal, factual, historical reading of Genesis chapter 2 is that women were created second as an afterthought by God and therefore occupy a secondary position in the order of creation.[3]

Women in the third group, as we are going to see below, are the proponents of the new trend in feminism in the country. Their studies and projects are of immense help in registering gender inequality in the texts of the Sacred Scriptures.[4] Still on this positive note, they are also able to highlight some significant but obscure roles of women in the Scripture. Some of these women in the third group who specialised in the study of the New Testament perceive the inseparability of the Old Testament and the New Testament. Thus they make meaningful use of the Old Testament as they expound the New Testament texts.[5]

SOCIAL BACKGROUND OF THE READERS

The responses of each group of readers differ according to their understanding of the Old Testament texts and their exposure to life in general. Before discussing these varied approaches of the Nigerian women to the Old Testament, I would like to mention some features of their cultural background that influence the way most of them view the Sacred Texts.

---

[3] R. Uchem, "Liberative Inculturation: The Case of Igbo Women," in *Nigeria Religion and Conflict Resolution* (Bulletin of Ecumenical Theology Vol. 14; Enugu: The Ecumenical Association of Nigerian Theologians, 2002), 94.

[4] Many works by women like Rose Uchem bear witness to this. One of her recent articles geared towards an honest search for the rights of women is entitled "Gender Equality from a Christian Perspective," in *Gender Equality from a Christian Perspective* (Enugu: Ifendu Publications, 2006), 43–56. She is also the editor of this collective work.

[5] T. Okure, who is cited in this work, has both taught and written quite extensively on the New Testament.

The society in which these women find themselves is chiefly patriarchal. In spite of the significant roles they play in their individual homes and in the society at large, women are still considered as belonging to a weaker gender. A man usually heads a family and a woman growing up in her father's house naturally prepares herself to leave the family and change her family name to that of her husband. This is because when she marries she belongs fully to the family of her husband and most often she inherits nothing from her paternal home. It is a society where an unmarried woman receives little or no respect; therefore every woman wishes to procure that honour, protection and respect which traditional marriage bestows on every married woman. In the case of the dissolution of the marriage, the children belong to their father. Although in our society today there is a strong presence of women leaders in some sectors of public life, the leaders of society remain predominantly men.

Some traditional laws evidently infringe on the rights of women.[6] In a difficult situation where both genders are involved, men often emerge unscathed. Women suffer even to the point of offering their lives. In the case of adultery, for instance, those mothers who have been abandoned by their husbands lack words to express their ordeal.

It is a society where widowers quickly take another life partner, while widows suffer human degradation from men and most painfully from other women.[7] A woman writing on the plight of widows articulates her view and observations as follows:

> A widower is free to marry as many times as he wishes, depending on how many times he lost his wife, but in the case of a widow she is forced by the sanctions imposed by the society to marry only a next-of-kin and in rare cases should she be allowed to marry outside her late husband's lineage. Whenever this situation of marriage outside the kindred occurs, it always has no approval of the late husband's kindred. Ironically, if a woman loses two husbands then she never gets another chance to marry because she is assumed to be a husband killer.[8]

---

[6] Some women, particularly those who read the Old Testament critically, aver that these traditional laws are against the message of the Bible. See e.g. D. N. Nwachukwu, "The Christian Widow in African Culture," in *The Will to Arise: Women, Tradition and the Church in Africa* (ed. M. A. Oduyoye and M. R. A. Kanyoro; New York: Orbis Books, 1992), 68.

[7] Cf. M. C. Nwaturuocha, *Widows in our Society* (Onitsha: Snaap, 2000), 21, includes a picture depicting some women, who are usually the close relations of a man, who were taunting their widowed sister-in-law in the name of tradition.

[8] C. U. Asogwa, *Widowhood, Human Dignity and Social Justice in Nigeria: A Biblical-Theological Study* (Enugu: Director, Development Education Centre, 1993), 23. Another work by the same author on the plight of women is *Women's struggle, Women's work: A Discussion Guide for Church Women's Group* (Ibadan: CARE-CAN Publishers, 1987).

It is a society where the oversight of women's dignity is often explained with reference to their so-called weakness. On the other hand, an apparent lack of bravery in a man makes onlookers deride him with phrases such as "You are behaving like a woman!" Thus a common connotation of the term "woman" is weakness.

Ironically, a society with such a strong patriarchal orientation counts so much on the strength of women in the families and in the society. The fast growing number of educated women in the society raises many of them to the status of permanent breadwinners of their families. This is because a large number of men opt for trading and its fluctuations in the country are often a source of an uncertain economic future. Educated women partners of these traders are less affected by fluctuating economic circumstances. Therefore, today most men look for women with a good academic background. These women sustain them in times of difficulties. In brief, the significant and indispensable roles of women in the society are overshadowed by the prevailing patriarchal attitudes. Such features are not absent in the Old Testament.

THE READERS' SOCIAL BACKGROUND IN RESPECT OF THE OLD TESTAMENT

With these traits of their background, Nigerian women readers of the Old Testament encounter in the Sacred Texts a cultural background that is not far removed from their own.

Why is Israel's originating history generally called the history of the patriarchs? Why is there such a strong overt patriarchal point of view among the narrators in the Bible? The narratives are usually told from the standpoint of men.

Besides Athaliah, who forced herself to the throne in the Kingdom of Judah, Israel had only men on its throne. In spite of the obviously significant roles of women in the Book of Judges, only Deborah is ranked among the "judges"; the rest of the charismatic deliverers in this book are all men.

The part that Eve played in the fall of human beings' primordial parents (Gen 3) is evoked in some Old Testament narratives. Great men in the history of Israel lost favour with God and humans because of the presence of women in their lives. In the story of Joseph the young slave in the house of Potiphar narrowly escaped the snares of his master's wife (Gen 39). Samson is introduced as a hero; the elaborate narrative on his birth that ushered his coming bears witness to this (Judg 13). That taint of weakness and depravity first exhibited by Eve accompanies her kind and in the life of Samson it is Delilah who became another man-betrayer (Judg 16). Bathsheba's relationship with David reduced the monarch to an adulterer (2 Sam 11), murderer and usurper. His family was eventually destabilised. Women lured the great and wise King Solomon from the true faith to pantheism (1 Kgs 11).

There are also instances of women tormenting other women. The dismissal of Hagar from the house of Abraham and Sarah appeared to be the best solution to the mental agony these two women were undoubtedly undergoing (Gen 21:8–21). Again, the childless Hannah did not find it easy with Peninah (1 Sam 1).

An inventory of such unconstructive depictions of women in the Bible can still continue, but a quick look at how some passages from the Book of Sirach (Ecclesiasticus)[9] presents this will highlight the picture vividly: "Do not give yourself to a woman and let her trample down your strength" (Sir 9:2). This is reminiscent of the dissolute Eve and her children, who were instrumental in the fall of "men of strength". Sirach 25:24 further expresses this sharply: "From a woman sin had its beginning, and because of her we all die". Another text compares both genders: "Better is the wickedness of a man than a woman who does good; it is the woman who brings shame and disgrace" (Sir 42:14). For similar texts in the Book of Sirach see Sira 9:3, 8; 25:13, 16, 21; and 42:13. Besides all these, the author of the Book of Ecclesiasticus has a beautiful ode to women (see Sir 26:13–18).

The part many women played in the history behind the Old Testament texts is sometimes emphasised. Those who composed the story of Moses underscored the importance of women in the life of Israel's leader. His father is barely mentioned at the beginning of the story (Exod 2:1); the rest of the narrative places women in the forefront. His mother and sister saved him from an untimely death to which other male children were destined. The daughter of his persecutor rescued Moses and adopted him. When he was fleeing for dear life, women helped him to find asylum and one of them, Zipporah, became his life partner (see Exod 2:11–22). The same Zipporah saved his life when he was again in danger (see Exod 4:24–26). In the same line with these brave women in the life of Moses are Deborah, a prophetess and a judge (see Judg 4–5), Judith and Esther. The faithful woman, Ruth, should also be mentioned for she paved the way for the royal lineage. These women played significant roles in the life of the Chosen People.[10]

THE READERS' VARIED RESPONSES TO THE OLD TESTAMENT

Nigerian women reading Old Testament texts find themselves reading stories that echo their life situations. Their reactions to their social background determine their internalisation of the message of the Sacred Texts. Here the three groups of readers mentioned above represent the three major different types of internalisations of the message of the Bible among Nigerian women.

---

[9] Though the Book of Sirach is not recognised by many Christians as canonical, it forms part of the Bible widely read and cited by many.

[10] A critical study of the roles of women in both the Old Testament and the New Testament is the main subject of a contribution by T. Okure, "Women in the Bible," in *With Passion and Compassion: Third World Women Doing Theology* (ed. V. Fabella and M. A. Oduyoye; Maryknoll, New York: Orbis, 1988), 47–59.

Those without formal education adhere strongly to the traditional views about women. They do not think that there should be changes in the societal structure. They are content with the situation and make little or no effort to effect reasonable changes. For these women the Old Testament texts contain other interesting things besides its positive or negative views about women. These include the mighty work of God in creation, his self-revelation, and the beautiful songs in the Psalms and in other parts of the Bible. The texts on the status and social depiction of women are received no differently from how this is perceived in their own culture. For them it is normal that revelations are made only to men who are the heads of families. Male superiority and the gender inequality prevalent in the Old Testament are part of the world's *sacred order*. An interesting point, and indeed a positive one, about women in this group is their childlike disposition towards, and their ardent faith in, the message of the Bible. Some passages are actually difficult to understand, especially those that challenge morality. Why should the dwellers of the land of Canaan be displaced or even exterminated because of the divine promise? But who can probe the mind of the Mighty God? He alone knows why this should be carried out.

Women in the second group have had a formal education but have not undertaken any in-depth study of the Bible. These are the ones who, in spite of the high level of education that some of them have acquired, are still considered as "women"—with all the connotations that this word evokes in the society—by their male counterparts. These are the ones who suffer unjustly at home, in their places of work and in society. Listening to the Scriptures and the explanations, and reading them in their private studies, many of them find themselves questioning the implications of some elements of their culture in these texts. Many of them do not go farther than this, especially the fervent believers among them. Their faith helps them to accept all this as part of God's plan for human salvation. However, they perceive traces of injustices and inequality in the presentation of women in the Sacred Texts.[11] They also see their role models in the characters of some women.[12] Hannah, the mother of Samuel, for instance, becomes a model of assiduous prayer and faith in God for whom nothing is impossible. Deborah, judge and prophetess, is a brave woman who challenged the men of her own time; she is worthy of emulation for she points to that equality for which many women in this group yearn. Ruth is a model of faithfulness and identification with other women in their sufferings. In the life of Ruth it is feasible for women to unite and achieve a common purpose. Women in the life of Moses are ideal mothers and models of what every woman should strive after. They are icons of tenderness and

---

[11] Biblical passages that mention God's solicitous attitude toward women are often treasured and cited in defense of the right of women in the society (cf. Nwaturuocha, *Widows in our Society*, 38–39).

[12] Asogwa, *Widowhood, Human Dignity and Social Justice*, 48–51, focusing on widows in the Old Testament, highlights the significant roles of these women in Ancient Israel.

compassion, characteristic of every woman. Finally the ode to '*eshet hayil* in Prov 31:10–31 is a treasured hymn reminiscent of similar sonnets in honour of women in the Nigerian culture.

The third group can be termed a privileged group because of their formal theological studies or specialisation in biblical studies. With regard to women's response to the Old Testament, these women can be divided into two groups: mild biblical scholars and leftist activists. There are in the first place the mild biblical scholars who endeavour to bring the message of the Sacred Texts to the people.[13] They are mainly teachers in higher institutions and writers on biblical issues. A positive approach to the Old Testament texts bears much fruit and allows room for constructive re-reading of some passages that might appear biased. Having acquired a better understanding of the social contexts of the biblical texts, these women read and expound on the Old Testament texts with much ease. Traditional practices that are reflected in the Sacred Texts are firmly addressed without raising much dust. The leftist activists, on the other hand, capitalise on their scholarship to liberate women from social degradation.[14] They follow a new trend of feminism that seeks to sensitise women sufficiently to assert themselves in society. As Bible experts they sometimes exaggerate the unfair portrayal of women in the Old Testament. One achieves little with anger and the outcome of the energy expended is not worth the effort. Even though these activists have succeeded in attracting sympathisers from the opposite gender, they often make greater enemies in the process. Often the message of the Bible is sidetracked in pursuit of the rights of women. Many noteworthy texts that emphasise the role of women are overlooked and much confusion is instilled in other women whose foothold in the faith is still feeble.

Conclusion

The socio-cultural background of the Nigerian women readers of the Old Testament has an influence on their understanding of the Sacred Texts. More enlightened groups among these readers perceive the features that the Old Testament setting has in common with their own culture and this affects their understanding of the Bible, both positively and negatively. The rapid increase in the

---

[13] See M. J. Obiorah, "You cannot do it alone (Exod 18,18): A Biblical Advice on Collaborative Ministry," in *Collaborative Ministry in the Context of Inculturation* (ed. I. M. C. Obinwa; Onitsha: Africana First Publishers, 2006), 35–45.

[14] See biblical citations in a work by R. M. Owanikiri, "The Priesthood of Church Women in the Nigerian Context," in *The Will to Arise: Women, Tradition and the Church in Africa* (ed. M. A. Oduyoye and M. R. A. Kanyoro; New York: Orbis Books, 1992), 206–219, particularly her interpretation of Gen 2:18 on page 213 of her chapter. She has a master's degree in New Testament Studies and at the time she wrote the article she was a lecturer at a Nigerian University.

level of literacy among women should also witness a corresponding increase in the number of those who study the Bible so as to help others accept the message of the Sacred Scriptures. This, we hope, will effect significant changes in those who already appropriate the Old Testament, sometimes wrongly, in their fight for the rights of women. A close reading of the Old Testament has elucidated the important roles of women in the history of the Ancient Israel. Many women are playing similar roles in Nigerian society and this should be a starting point in our honest quest for the rights of women.

Part III

CONSEQUENCES

The Global Context and Its Consequences for Old Testament Interpretation

LOUIS C. JONKER

INTRODUCTION: WHO AM I?

My participation in a session on *global* hermeneutics is for me no small occasion. Coming from the southern tip of the African continent as well as from a very specific part of South African biblical scholarship (namely white, male scholarship) makes my inclusion in this seminar no self-evident decision. My social location could potentially have silenced my voice in any debate on global hermeneutics. I am well aware of the fact that any voice with a more Western inclination advocating a global hermeneutics could very easily be interpreted as another imperialising or colonising endeavour. It seems to me that the term "global hermeneutics" has different overtones in traditional Western scholarship, on the one hand, and non-traditional scholarship in non-Western and marginal contexts, on the other hand.[1]

I am starting my contribution with this ideological-critical appraisal of my own participation, because I am convinced that we cannot (and may not!) talk of global hermeneutics if we do not know ourselves.[2] It seems to me that issues of identity cannot be separated from our discussions on global hermeneutics. In an international conference at my university early in 2006 which was intended to bring African and European scholarship into conversation around the theme "Exegesis and Actualisation", I was challenged to reflect on my own identity as a biblical scholar.[3] There I shared from my own biography the fact that I am living in different worlds simultaneously. Because of my more Western training as a biblical scholar, I have come to appreciate the rigour of traditional Western scholarship. But

---

[1] Ukpong, for example, emphasises in his work that for a long time in the history of biblical scholarship globalisation has been a vehicle for the propagation of European and American interpretations. See J. Ukpong, "Developments in Biblical Interpretation in Africa: Historical and Hermeneutical Directions," in *The Bible in Africa: Transactions, Trajectories and Trends* (eds. G. O. West and M. W. Dube; Leiden: Brill, 2000), 11–28.

[2] See R. C. Bailey, "The danger of ignoring one's own cultural bias in interpreting the text," in *The Postcolonial Bible* (ed. R. S. Sugirtharajah; Sheffield: Sheffield Academic Press, 1998), 66–90.

[3] See L. C. Jonker, "Living in different worlds simultaneously. Or: A plea for contextual integrity," in *African and European Readers of the Bible in Dialogue: In Quest of a Shared Meaning* (eds. J. H. de Wit and G. O. West; Leiden: Brill, 2008), 107–119.

being born and bred on the African continent, I also have great appreciation for the sensitivity of African biblical scholarship to flesh-and-blood contexts (such as poverty, oppression and the HIV/Aids pandemic) within which the Bible is interpreted. My identity as a biblical scholar and reader of the Bible is a quilt of different—sometimes harmonious and sometimes conflicting—dimensions.

My contribution in this seminar stems from this hybrid identity that I am—an identity that I have come to accept and that I would like to nurture. I therefore also call on you to interpret my contribution within this condition of hybridity.

REDEFINING "GLOBAL CONTEXT"?

I would like to start my contribution by reflecting on our understanding of "the global context" that determines our global hermeneutics. It seems to me that in the literature and in our deliberations here "global" is often understood as "contemporary geography"—an understanding which seeks the locus of our interpretations exclusively in the fact that we live in different parts of the world. Our seminar session was introduced by a paper exploring the geographical and institutional aspects of global Old Testament studies (Holter). The case studies that followed were presentations from different parts of the world—Africa, Latin America, Asia and Europe—and deliberately so. These perspectives are, of course, indispensable and valuable for our understanding of and discussions on global hermeneutics.

However, I am wondering whether we should not widen our understanding of "global context" by also including a temporal dimension in our definitions.[4] Our understanding of "global" lets us ask the question: how should we interpret the Bible together with our brothers and sisters all over the world? And rightly so! However, should we not also include a temporal perspective which makes us aware that we are not only interpreting the Bible together with our brothers and sisters, but that we also do so in conversation with our mothers and fathers? Should we not show greater awareness that all contemporary interpretative communities are embedded in traditions of interpretation?

---

[4] I deliberately avoid the terms "synchrony" and "diachrony" here, because these notions are often misunderstood within a dichotomy which puts them in opposition to, and in tension with, one another. See L. C. Jonker, "Reading with one eye closed? Or: What you miss when you do not read biblical texts multidimensionally," *OTE* 19/1 (2006), 58–76. See also J. Barr, "The Synchronic, the Diachronic and the Historical: A Triangular Relationship?" in *Synchronic or Diachronic? A debate on method in Old Testament exegesis* (ed. J. C. De Moor; OTS 34; Leiden: Brill), 1–14; D. J. A. Clines, "Beyond Synchronic/Diachronic," in *Synchronic or Diachronic? A debate on method in Old Testament exegesis* (ed. J. C. De Moor; OTS 34; Leiden: Brill), 52–71.

It seems to me that Prof. Ukpong's contribution also wanted to emphasise this point.[5] He has identified three phases in the open-ended *process* of globalisation that started long ago. With this approach he has emphasised that we cannot speak of global hermeneutics without taking into account that we are all part of a *process*. There is thus a temporal aspect that should be considered in our deliberations. We should become aware of where in this process our discussions are situated. I would like to acknowledge the value of this input into our debate.

However, I would like to append to his temporal approach the suggestion that the traditions of interpretation that I am talking about could be described in broader terms than merely reducing them to the opposition between Western and non-Western approaches. It seems to me that if we persist to work with a conflict model in our descriptions of the road that all of us have travelled thus far, we will not come to an appreciation of our different approaches.

All interpretations, Western or non-Western, are contextual. That means that all our interpretations and approaches have developed against the background of real life thought patterns, cultural environments, physical and spiritual needs. Without being aware of how our unique approaches have developed, we will not only be unable to identify our own strengths, but also our own weaknesses.

I would like to argue that the resistance to European and American control by non-Westerners (i.e. the third phase that Ukpong has identified) has nothing to do with those approaches themselves. This point has been confirmed by Ukpong in other publications,[6] as well as by Zinkuratire,[7] Mojola[8] and other scholars, who argue that traditional Western models of biblical interpretation (such as historical-critical or socio-cultural scholarship) can offer much to African interpretations. The resistance of which Ukpong is speaking is rather against the power relations that regulate our interpretative endeavours in a global context (and I will come back to this issue later in my contribution). We should not in our reaction against power relations ignore the inherent strengths and weaknesses of our different approaches. And those inherent strengths and weaknesses can only become apparent to us when we consider our respective traditions of interpretation, and when we bring our own traditions into dialogue with other traditions. We need a temporal perspective on our interpretative endeavours in order to salvage a global hermeneutics from the

---

[5] Although Prof. Ukpong was also invited to participate in the session in Ljubljana, he could unfortunately not attend the conference. My response in this paper is to the abstract that he submitted.

[6] E.g. J. S. Ukpong, "Can African Old Testament scholarship escape the historical critical approach?" in *Newsletter on African Old Testament Scholarship* 7 (1999), 2–5.

[7] V. Zinkuratire, "Method and relevance in African Biblical interpretation" (Stellenbosch: Unpublished paper read at the International workshop on Old and New Testament studies in Africa, 1999).

[8] A. Mojola, "The Social Sciences and the study of the Old Testament in Africa: Some methodological considerations," in *Interpreting the Old Testament in Africa* (eds. M. Getui *et al.*; Nairobi: Acton Press, 2001), 89–99.

oppositional mode in which it is often articulated. Our problem is not the diversity of interpretations that we come up with in our globalised world and the multitude of approaches that we are using. The problem is rather the exclusivist claims that we make from our respective contexts and the power plays that we keep alive in our hermeneutical endeavours.[9]

In order to avoid any misunderstanding, let me be a little more specific on how our traditions of interpretation should be involved in our hermeneutic theories: I argued in my introductory paragraph that a discussion on global hermeneutics cannot be separated from the issue of identity. However, it is not only through interaction with contemporary interpretative communities that we get to know ourselves, but also through interaction with those who have gone before us in our own traditions. We all stand on the shoulders of those who have gone before us in our respective contexts. However, we are doing so critically. When we include the earlier stages in our own traditions of interpretation in our reflection on our hermeneutical task, we not only discover our continuities with the past, but also our discontinuities and differentiations. We then get a better perspective on our own strengths, but also on our deficiencies and weaknesses. We also get a better understanding of why almost all of us—I would guess—have hybrid identities. Exactly because of an increasingly globalised world, the lines of our traditions of interpretation have started intertwining. Without a temporal perspective in our discussions on global hermeneutics, we will remain unaware of this fact.

CONSEQUENCES FOR OLD TESTAMENT INTERPRETATION IN A GLOBAL CONTEXT

Let me now try to show some consequences of such a view for Old Testament interpretation in a global context. I would like to argue that at least the aspects listed below should be prioritised in a global hermeneutics.

TAKING OUR HERMENEUTICAL CUES FROM THE PROCESSES OF (RE)INTERPRETATION IN THE OLD TESTAMENT ITSELF

We are all well aware of the fact that the Old Testament is not a monolithic block of literature stemming from just one theological tradition. A diversity of traditions was included in the Old Testament canon, without annihilating the multitude of voices. These traditions were interacting with one another and reinterpreting one another. I have argued elsewhere[10] that textual production and

---

[9] See L. C. Jonker, *Exclusivity and Variety. Perspectives on Multidimensional Exegesis* (Kampen: Kok-Pharos, 1996).

[10] See *idem*, "Communities of faith as texts in the process of Biblical interpretation," *Skrif en Kerk* 20/1 (1999), 79–92; Jonker, "Reading with one eye closed?"; L. C. Jonker and

textual reception in the time of origin of the Old Testament should not be seen as separate processes. Certain contexts of origin brought forth textual traditions that were transmitted to subsequent generations. The reception of these traditions by the subsequent generations in their changed circumstances often sparked off further processes of textual production. Textual reception therefore gave rise to renewed textual production. In this process we observe the courage to reinterpret and to adapt. We see biblical writers prepared to take from the past, but also to differentiate from the past.

The Books of Chronicles are probably prime examples of this hermeneutic.[11] The processes of interpretation during the Chronicler's age were certainly not merely a repetition of the past. They rather reflect the deep hermeneutical presupposition that understanding is never finished. The re-appropriation of their older historical and cultic traditions stood in the service of identity formation in changed and changing circumstances. I have indicated elsewhere[12] that "(t)his observation warns against the type of interpretation that remains oriented to the past, without giving account for the circumstances of the present." To make this applicable for our discussion on global hermeneutics: a global hermeneutics should be able to include not only those interpretations and approaches that emphasise the pre-stages of the Old Testament texts and the world behind those texts, but also those approaches that want to relate those biblical traditions to present-day realities and contexts. I have furthermore argued that the opposite position is certainly also

---

D. G. Lawrie, *Fishing for Jonah (anew). Various approaches to biblical interpretation* (Stellenbosch: African Sun Media, 2005).

[11] See L. C. Jonker, *Reflections of King Josiah in Chronicles. Late stages of the Josiah Reception in 2 Chr 34f* (Gütersloh: Gütersloher Verlag, 2003); idem, "The rhetorics of finding a new identity in a multi-cultural and multi-religious society," *Verbum et Ecclesia* 24/2 (2003), 396–416; idem, "The Cushites in the Chronicler's version of Asa's Reign: A Secondary Audience in Chronicles?", *OTE* 19/3 (2006), 863–881; idem, "Reforming history: The hermeneutical significance of the Books of Chronicles," *VT* 57/1 (2007), 21–44; idem, "Refocusing the battle accounts of the kings: Identity formation in the Books of Chronicles," in *Behutsames Lesen. Alttestamentliche Exegese im Gespräch mit Literaturwissenschaft und Kulturwissenschaften* (eds. S. Lubs et al.; Leipzig: Evangelische Verlagsanstalt, 2007), 245–274; idem, "Who constitutes society? Yehud's self-understanding in the Late Persian Era as reflected in the Books of Chronicles," *JBL* 127/4 (2008), 707–728; idem, "The disappearing Nehushtan: The Chronicler's reinterpretation of Hezekiah's reformation measures," in *From Ebla to Stellenbosch* (eds. I. Cornelius and L. C. Jonker; ADPV 37; Wiesbaden: Harrassowitz, 2008), 116–140; idem, "The Chronicler's Portrayal of Solomon as the King of Peace within the Context of the International Peace Discourses of the Persian era", *OTE* 21/3 (2008), 653–669; idem, "The Chronicler and the prophets. Who were his authoritative sources?", *SJOT* 22/2 (2008), 271–292; idem, "Textual Identities in the Books of Chronicles: The Case of Jehoram's History," in *Community Identity in Judean Historiography. Biblical and Comparative Perspectives* (eds. G. N. Knoppers and K. A. Ristau; Winona Lake, ID.: Eisenbrauns), 197–217.

[12] See idem, "Reforming history," 37.

true: "It [i.e. the observation of reinterpretation and adaptation in the biblical traditions—LCJ] warns against interpretation that orients itself only to the present, without taking into account the past." This implies that a global hermeneutics should be able to contextualise the biblical texts in contemporary contexts, without severing or ignoring the ties with past traditions.

The transformative potential of the Old Testament texts can in my view only be unlocked in a global hermeneutics if there is a healthy interaction between past and present in our interpretative endeavours. A concentration on the here and now in biblical interpretation could blind our eyes to the transformative discourse into which we enter when interpreting biblical traditions.

THE VALUE OF STUDYING THE *WIRKUNGSGESCHICHTE* OF SPECIFIC TEXTS

In the previous point I concentrated on the long and varied processes that led to the development of the Old Testament. In this section I would like to focus on the traditions of interpretation that were generated by the Old Testament canon subsequent to its finalisation. Let me illustrate by means of an example: we are certainly all aware of the eventful *Wirkungsgeschichte* of a text such as the so-called Curse of Ham in Gen 9. Many commentators have shown how this text was abused throughout history from various ideological perspectives.[13] This text was used in the history of interpretation to condemn black Africans to becoming second-class citizens, to legitimise slavery and colonialism on a global scale and, not least, to bolster apartheid in South Africa. A global hermeneutics that does not take note of this long *Wirkungsgeschichte* will be prone to repeat the misuses of the past.

We all know of biblical texts that have exerted a similar influence to Gen 9. In the South African context, for example, a very specific interpretation of the Tower of Babel narrative in Gen 11 formed the biblical basis of apartheid theology.[14] The Book of Exodus, on the other hand, functioned prominently in liberation theology circles. We know of those texts that were (and are!) used to justify the oppression of women, and those that are used in many conservative churches to condemn homosexuality as a sin. A global hermeneutics has the ethical responsibility to uncover and expose the *Wirkungsgeschichte* of those texts.

THE VALUE OF INTERCULTURAL HERMENEUTICS

A third consequence of our view on global hermeneutics that I would like to highlight is the inevitability of intercultural hermeneutics. According to accepted

---

[13] See e.g. G. Wittenberg, "'... Let Canaan be his slave.' (Gen. 9:26) Is Ham also cursed?," *JThSA* 74 (1991), 46–56.

[14] See L. C. Jonker, "The biblical legitimization of ethnic diversity in Apartheid Theology," *Scriptura* 77 (2001), 165–183.

anthropological definitions, "intercultural" refers to communication between people from different cultures. It goes further than a mere acceptance or acknowledgement of multiculturality.[15] Intercultural hermeneutics therefore takes its point of departure in the interaction, the communication between different cultures. One should, however, distinguish at least two different levels of intercultural exchange in biblical hermeneutics:[16]

(i) When contemporary readers of the Bible read it from their respective modern socio-cultural environments, they often feel estranged because of the socio-cultural distance between ancient (biblical) and modern contexts. The reading of the Bible in contemporary contexts (be they Western or non-Western) is therefore, by implication, an intercultural encounter.

(ii) However, when contemporary readers from different socio-cultural contexts read the Bible *together* (as in a global hermeneutics), this creates another level of intercultural encounter. There is then a double estrangement: because of the distance described in the first point, as well as because of the socio-cultural distance between different contemporary environments and traditions of interpretation.

The second level of interculturality concerns us in a quest for a global hermeneutics. However, I would like to argue that sensitivity to the first level of intercultural exchange could be of great value for our reflection on the second level. In this regard socio-historical studies have offered many valuable perspectives on the socio-cultural, socio-political and socio-economic contexts of the origin of the biblical writings. These insights have developed our hermeneutical sophistication in dealing with texts stemming from another cultural environment.[17]

Taking our cues from those developments in biblical hermeneutics we could start exploring the dynamics of intercultural exchange on a global scale. It could help us to avoid the dangers of reductionism and essentialism when interacting with biblical scholars from all over the world and their interpretations. It could sensitise us to the unique contribution that all the participants in global hermeneutics bring to the interpretation process.

INVITATION TO A LIMINAL SPACE

Now that I have shown the consequences of the widening of our definition of "global context" to include a temporal dimension, I will close with a section in

---

[15] See *idem*, "On becoming a family: Multiculturality and Interculturality in South Africa," in *Expository Times* 118/10 (2007), 480–487.
[16] See my discussion in *idem*, "Jesus among the ancestors. Continuity and discontinuity," in *Through the eyes of another. Intercultural reading of the Bible* (eds. J. H. de Wit *et al.*; Elkhart, Indiana: Institute of Mennonite Studies, 2004), 322.
[17] See Ukpong's view on inculturation in J. S. Ukpong, "Rereading the Bible with African eyes: Inculturation and hermeneutics," *JThSA* 91 (1995), 3–14.

which I would like to suggest an exegetical model which could be helpful for doing biblical interpretation in a global context.

I have argued in many previous publications that a multidimensional approach to biblical interpretation can help us escape the looming dangers of exclusivity in our global exegetical endeavours. A multidimensional approach wants to steer away from exclusivism, advocating the adoption of another attitude in biblical interpretation. This alternative attitude is one of communality.[18]

We (especially those of us trained in a Western model of scholarship) value individuality in biblical scholarship. Individual scholars specialise in certain textual corpora, exegetical methods, or related fields of study. And from these positions of individuality we try to make our contributions to biblical scholarship. Actually, we should rather speak of biblical "scholarships". Many conferences bear witness to the fact that there is no communality in our hermeneutical endeavours. Rather, it seems that we all compete to win some or other coveted prize. Should we not try to create a liminal space of communality before any dialogue can start?

I have expressed this elsewhere[19] as follows: "In a communal approach the desideratum is to keep striving for contextual integrity. Contextual integrity can be achieved where justice is done to each one of the different contextualities involved in the process of biblical interpretation. Or, to put it in the inverse: Contextual integrity cannot be achieved where one type of contextuality is over-emphasised to the detriment of other types of contextuality. The communality of the approach suggested here opens up the liminal space where scholars with different life interests can start sharing their scholarship on the different interpretative interests involved. Or to put it in yet another way: A communal approach moves away from the binary oppositions that the quest for contextual authenticity would necessitate. When contextual authenticity[20] is the norm, it is inevitable that interpretive contextuality (i.e. who I am) and didactic contextuality (i.e. for whom I am interpreting) should coincide. Within this scheme of thinking these two types of contextuality are either in congruence, or they are not. ... A communal approach would rather appeal to the diversity of ... scholars to come to the liminal space of community in order to share, to contradict, to influence, to change one another's interests in terms of the whole spectrum of contextualities involved in biblical interpretation. Within such a community of biblical scholarship the individual interpreter (of African origin or otherwise) could interact with one another on the

---

[18] See Jonker, *Exclusivity and Variety*; idem, "Towards a 'communal' approach for reading the Bible in Africa," in *Interpreting the Old Testament in Africa* (eds. Getui et al.; Nairobi: Acton Press, 2001), 77–88; idem, "'Contextuality' in (South) African exegesis: Reflections on the communality of our exegetical methodologies," *OTE* 18/3 (2005), 637–650; idem, "Reading with one eye closed?"; Jonker and Lawrie, *Fishing for Jonah (anew)*.

[19] See Jonker, "Contextuality", 644–645.

[20] See J. N. K. Mugambi, "African and Africanist Scholarship," *BOTSA* 14 (2003), 9–12.

basis of the inter-contextuality involved in our common pursuit of biblical interpretation."

This view takes its point of departure in the dialogical nature of meaning. Meaning is not something "out there" which can be excavated from those authoritative texts that we have at our disposal. Those with the most efficient tools (read: money and methods)[21] are obviously the fastest in uncovering "meaning". And this *Vorsprung durch Technik* (to borrow an expression from the advertising campaign of a well-known German car) puts these interpreters in a position of dominance and power. Certain perspectives and approaches (or interpretative contexts) are simply regarded as being more valid and important than others. However, when we start acknowledging that meaning is not something "out there", but that it is rather something dialogical that comes into being in interaction with others, the issue of dominance or interpretative power could be relativised. No one of us can claim sole possession of meaning. Without interaction, there is no meaning. Possession of meaning leads to relativism (where each one claims the validity of his/her point of view). Meaning-as-interaction, however, provides contours along which the ethical responsibility of global hermeneutics could be fulfilled.

My proposal of a communal approach is not an attempt at formulating yet another exegetical (super-)method. It should rather be seen as an appreciation of the multidimensionality of the textual traditions that we consider authoritative, as well as of the multidimensionality of the global world in which we interpret those traditions. The attitude of communality could bring us to that liminal space where different approaches and different contexts can start interacting with one another in a dialogical uncovering of meaning.

Conclusion

I am in complete agreement with Ukpong's analysis of the three phases in the process of the globalisation of Old Testament studies. And I agree that we are now in the third phase in which resistance to European and American control of Old Testament interpretation is offered by non-Westerners and in which the decentralisation of interpretation is taking place. But I would like to remain an idealist who looks forward to a fourth phase: a phase of communality. This fourth phase will not be characterised by binary oppositions and power plays. Our exegetical agenda will then be set by the biblical texts themselves, and not by our agendas of control and influence.

---

[21] See K. Holter, "It's not only a question of money! African Old Testament scholarship between the myths and meaning of the South and the money and methods of the North," *OTE* 11 (1998), 240–254.

Will a fourth phase ever dawn? Probably not! But this does not prevent me from remaining an idealist!

The Global Context and Its Consequences for Old Testament Translation

ALOO MOJOLA

INTRODUCTION

The first translation of the Bible in any language is always a momentous experience. It gives people a sense of God finally speaking in their own language, the language of their heart and mind. It makes the Scriptures available and accessible and makes it possible for people to hear the God of Abraham and of our Lord Jesus Christ speak to them in their own mother tongues and through the prism of their own cultures and traditions.

In the Western world the process of translation, production and distribution of the Scriptures in the native languages of Europe is usually taken for granted. It is easily forgotten that it was the sacrifices of Bible translators such as Jerome, Wycliffe, Tyndale, Martin Luther and others that lay at the root of the transformation of the church, especially in the movement that has come to be referred to as the Protestant Reformation and the Christian revivals that were associated with it. The new translations that resulted in the various national and ethnic languages of Europe encapsulated the new Protestant spirit and defended the right and need of every people to understand the Scriptures in their own language. Translation democratised access to the Christian Scriptures and broke the monopoly of the priest and the missionary. It opened the way for fresh interpretations of the Holy Scriptures by individuals and communities that challenged the status quo. It contributed to the development of a new hermeneutic with its own dynamics.

It is common knowledge that the Judeo-Christian Holy Scriptures were originally written in the Hebrew, Aramaic and Greek tongues. Without the work of translators the Holy Scriptures would be virtually a closed book for the majority of those who accept them and receive them as the authoritative and inspired Word of God. No wonder translation has always been at the cutting edge of the Christian mission. Translation created and opened the possibilities for cross-cultural and cross-religious communication and dialogue to take place. Translation made it possible for the Gospel to cross new frontiers and open new mission fields.

Some have interpreted this as an aspect of the incarnation, a process that is facilitated when the Gospel is allowed to use the local idiom, or understood through the thought forms of the local culture, or seen through the prism or eyes of the vernacular. This process is sometimes referred to as the inculturation or the contextualisation of the Gospel in the cultures and everyday life of indigenous peoples.

Through Bible translation the Holy Scriptures are therefore functioning within a global environment where boundaries, geographical and cultural, have been crossed. In order to understand this context better we have to take a closer look at the phenomenon of globalisation. We do this with reference to Alex MacGillivray's *A Brief History of Globalisation—the Untold Story of Our Incredible Shrinking Planet.*[1]

GLOBALISATION AND ITS IMPLICATIONS

Globalisation is certainly not a new phenomenon. It has ancient roots. It is grounded on an imperial desire to expand one's wings and hegemonic control to an ever-widening circle, with the intent of bringing the other and all their worldly goods and treasures into one's own sphere of influence and power. MacGillivray[2] focuses on the essence of globalisation as involving not just "global scope" but "global intent" as well. Global intent is understood as "the ambition to encompass the whole planet". It includes a strong interest in trade, labour, finance and ideas as well as such key activities as religion, language, culture, sport and communication. It involves what he describes as critical planet-shrinking moments and events—commercial, social, financial, cultural and technological—that have markedly and rapidly shrunk the world into our present "global village" (Marshall McLuhan). The voyages of Christopher Columbus, Vasco da Gama and Ferdinand Magellan heralded a high point in the process of globalisation, as did the spice trade and the global commodities trade, "beginning with spices in the fifteenth century and following the transformation from three East India Companies through to today's 60,000 multinational corporations. Brazilian pepper is now sold to Indian immigrants under a British brand with a German name by a US company with an Irish name. That is globalisation in a nutshell".[3] While that early quest for spices involved risky voyages to the East, "who could have predicted that chicken tikka massala would one day become an every-day dinner dish in Britain?"[4]

McGillivray is right in asserting that globalisation is neither exclusively dominated by the American empire, nor exclusively the creation of the British Empire. Rather, as MacGillivray suggests, "Many of the building blocs of globalisation turn out to be French: *laissez-faire* economics, *pommes frites*, the passport, the metric system, the Suez canal, the round-the-world trip, FIFA and the Olympics, Minitel, Louis Vuitton.... And it's not just the French who have had

---

[1] See A. MacGillivray, *A Brief History of Globalisation: The Untold Story of our Incredible Shrinking Planet* (London: Constable and Robinson Ltd, 2006).
[2] *Ibid.*, 7.
[3] *Ibid.*, 8.
[4] *Ibid.*, 93.

global ambitions: we find unique contributions from many other cultures and nations—Greek, Mongol, Islamic, Chinese, Dutch, Irish...."[5] McGillivray acknowledges both the positive and the negative aspects of globalisation, the progressive as well as the destructive.

The first use of the word "global" in this sense has been traced to a *Harper's Magazine* article of 1892 which describes a Monsieur de Vogue, a Frenchman who "loves travel, he goes to the East and to the West for colors and ideas, his interests are as wide as the universe, his ambition, to use a word of his own, is to be 'global'".[6] Clearly it is not the drive to experience exotic "colours and ideas" a la Vogue that drove the globalisation process. This may be part of it. It was and is, however, fuelled by the capitalistic profit motive as well as its inextricably linked demand for technological innovation and development. The institutionalisation of science and the knowledge industry is a concomitant part of this process. The capitalistic profit motive continues to create the material conditions and to justify the need for the requisite infrastructure of the imperial enterprise and the globalisation process. It fuels and encourages the movement of peoples, be they migrants or slaves, hunters for gold or the pursuers of fame, explorers or mere travellers, the search for luxury goods—spices, sugar, tea, rubber, the creation of global supply chains, of colonies and empires, of transnational corporations, of the modern communication revolution that has given rise to the railway and the car, the jet plane and space-rocket, the traditional telephone and the mobile phone, the transistor radio and the TV, the calculator and the modern hand-held computer devices, the maxim gun and the nuclear bomb. The juice that ensures that the process remains sustainable has been "money, oil and the global casino."[7]

Against the background of the above discussion, it is an irony that the spread of Christianity—which is nothing short of a miracle—can partly be understood in terms of the phenomenon of globalisation. Christianity came into being during the period of the Roman Empire. The entire Mediterranean world was under the influence of the so-called *pax Romana* (Roman peace), Roman rule, and Roman hegemony. The movement of peoples and ideas across the empire undoubtedly facilitated the movement of ordinary Christians as well as professional Christian missionaries, such as the ones described in the book of the Acts of the Apostles of Jesus of Nazareth. The missionary journeys of the Apostle Paul described both in this book and some of his letters attest to his brilliant use of the infrastructure and superstructure of the Roman Empire.

---

[5] *Ibid.*, 11.
[6] *Ibid.*, 10.
[7] *Ibid.*, 186.

TRANSLATION, HERMENEUTICS AND THE GLOBAL CONTEXT

What are the implications of this history and the context of globalisation for the translation of the Bible? Translation involves a transfer of meaning from one language to another, from one culture to another, from one world to another, from one time period to another, from one belief system to another, etc. all at once. It is not simply translating words or sentences, but making sense of texts through a process of interpretation and understanding, of capturing the message of the source text and rendering it, as they say, accurately or faithfully in a receptor/target text. This is a complex hermeneutical exercise. In the process of such a transfer, the translator can make certain translation decisions or interventions. The translator makes decisions related to the target audience, the language level, the language type, the function or skopos of the translation, the question of the original text and, if there are variants, which variant to use, whether there are other translation versions of the text being translated and what role these will play in the new translation being undertaken. These and a myriad other decisions must be taken by the translator(s). In doing so, they need to bear in mind the needs of the sponsor(s) of the translation, the particular ideology or theological stance of the sponsor(s), their values and preferences, among other considerations. Questions of fidelity or faithfulness are important, yet they are not independent of the above considerations. Indeed the whole question of the ethics of translation is influenced by these considerations. The translator does not and cannot work in a vacuum or in some rarefied objective world free of any interests. In short, Bible translation takes place in contexts which are fully part of the dynamic global world.

In the case of the Old Testament there is the translator's relationship to the text, the translator's location in the faith community and the community's relationship and understanding of the text, or the place, role and function of the text in the life of the community. It is also important to take into account the faith community's relationship to the larger community to which they belong to, but which may not attach any significance to the text in question. This dialectic between the translator, the source text, the faith community that sustains the text, those in the community who commission or sponsor the translation of the text, the larger world—in all its diversity and plurality, etc.—of which the faith community is only a part, certainly plays a key role in this whole process. Translation is never neutral. It is subject to the problem of the partiality and limitations of the translators, their knowledge of the source text and its backgrounds (geographical, historical, social, cultural, linguistic, religious, political, etc.) and their knowledge of the target/receptor text and its backgrounds (geographical, historical, social, cultural, linguistic, religious, political, etc). Questions of power, of perspective, of pluralism/diversity, of interests, preferences, of identity, among others, play a crucial role. These considerations bear on the translators' understanding, interpretation and choices. Their command of the receptor/target language and their ability to express themselves in it does bear on the general quality of the translation.

Missionary translations—for example, on the African continent (my context)—were certainly indispensable in the transmission and appropriation of the faith in the diverse languages and cultures in their areas of missionary outreach. One would have expected these translations to faithfully convey missionary interpretations of the faith but, strangely, indigenous or mother-tongue speakers of these translations did not always derive the same intended readings or interpretations from these translations—occasionally resulting in readings or interpretations that ran counter to missionary dogma. Sanneh has observed that the "missionary adoption of the vernacular, therefore, was tantamount to adopting indigenous cultural criteria for the message, a piece of radical indigenisation far greater than the standard portrayal of mission as Western cultural imperialism".[8] It is therefore not surprising that some of these tended to be subversive of the received missionary confessional or denominational creeds. This may have been the cause of much conflict and even schism. The rise of the African independent churches is often linked to this reality. Translation opened up a Pandora's box. The notion of one authoritative official reading of the biblical text was no longer tenable. The Sacred Word was in a common tongue—of which the mother-tongue speakers were the final arbiters, and every speaker trusted his own reading and interpretation. The missionary could no longer have the final word, since God speaks directly to every reader of the Word in their own language. Translation thus empowered and liberated the local reader, even those without adequate preparation and understanding of biblical backgrounds. Translation made possible the rise of a distinctive form of African Christianity steeped in African culture and traditions. Elizabeth Isichei notes that this phenomenon and the independent churches inspired by it has "enriched not only African Christianity, but Christendom as a whole by the richness and creativity of their liturgies, and by their exploration of an insight that the West has often lost sight of but is now rediscovering: the unity of health of mind and body".[9]

The complexity of translating the Bible in the global context which has become obvious from the discussion above will now be illustrated with reference to two case studies.

---

[8] Sanneh, *Translating the Message*, 3.
[9] E. Isichei, *A History of Christianity in Africa* (Grand Rapids, Michigan: Eerdmans, 1995), 253.

OLD TESTAMENT TRANSLATION AND THE CASE OF THE IRAQW BIBLE: TWO CASE STUDIES

TRANSLATING THE NAME OF GOD IN THE IRAQW LANGUAGE AND CULTURE[10]

The Iraqw of Tanzania are to be found in the Mbulu district of Tanzania, not far from the famous Ngorongoro Crater and in the vicinity of the great Serengeti national park. They belong to the Southern Cushitic language group of the larger Afro-Asiatic family. The Iraqw speakers currently number around half a million people or a little more. They are mainly farmers and cattle keepers. Their Datooga and Maasai neighbours are a predominantly nomadic cattle people who are slowly adapting to a sedentary lifestyle in a generally dry environment. The Iraqw have practised their traditional religion for millennia. Christianity is a recent arrival in the Iraqw universe, dating to sometime in the first half of the twentieth century. The missionaries who introduced Christianity to the Iraqw were mainly Lutherans from Norway and Sweden as well as Catholics from elsewhere in Europe. Despite attempts to learn and use the local language, these missionaries tended to promote the use of the Kiswahili language and the Kiswahili Bible.

One of the challenges in translating the Iraqw Bible was the problem of translating the name for God. In the New Testament translation which was published in 1977 by the Bible Society of Tanzania a decision was made to borrow the Swahili Bantu name for God, i.e. Mungu. The indigenous and traditional Iraqw name for God, namely Looa, was thought to be unsuitable. The main justification for this change was explained to me by some key figures of the Iraqw New Testament translation team. The problem was that in Iraqw tradition and usage, Looa, the creator of the world and the giver of life, is believed to be female. Looa is referred to as the mother of all and the source of life. The femininity of Looa is captured in the Iraqw linguistic gender system, which has three gender markers. In this system the first group includes singular male animates, while the second group includes singular female animates. The third group is predominately made up of plurals. Non-animates fall in any of the three groups.

Even though according to the Iraqw worldview, Looa the creator God has most of the positive moral attributes ascribed to the Christian God, the translation team felt at the time that Looa's "femininity" is incompatible with the God of the Bible believed to be "masculine" in the Judaeo-Christian tradition. The team therefore decided to borrow from the Kiswahili language and culture, the dominant lingua franca in the region. God's name in Kiswahili, namely Mungu, is not gender

---

[10] This first case is based on my work as a translation consultant with this team for a period of more than ten years. Parts of this study are based on a paper entitled "A 'Female' God in East Africa—or the Problem of translating God's Name among the Iraqw of Mbulu, Tanzania", originally prepared for a UBS Translation Triennial Workshop held in Chiang Mai, Thailand, 8–25, May 1994 and included in the *UBS Bulletin* 170/171 (1994), 87–93.

specific. It only places Mungu in the class of persons. Kiswahili is basically a Bantu language which is widely spoken in East and Central Africa by over fifty million speakers. The indigenous Waswahili people live along the East African coast and are predominantly Islamic. It is of interest that in the course of the Islamisation of the Waswahili people, during which time Kiswahili borrowed many terms from Arabic, the Kiswahili term for God, Mungu, remained untouched even in normal Muslim Kiswahili discourse. Farouk M. Topan, an East African Swahili scholar, has observed that "(a)lmost all major terms for an Islamic discourse in Swahili are derived from Arabic".[11] He suggests that this process of borrowing Islamic or Arabic terms or concepts took one or more of three paths, which he presents as: "(i) the original Arabic term was Swahilised, e.g. Ruh (Ar.) → roho (Sh.), (ii) the original Arabic term was Swahilised and, additionally, given Bantu synonym, e.g. rasul (Ar.)→ rasuli/mtume (Sw.), (iii) the original Arabic term was generally not adopted but the concept was given a Swahili term".[12]

Topan cites God's name in Swahili as illustrating the third process. He agrees that "Allah has not taken root as such in ordinary Swahili religious parlance, except in theological formulae (Qur'anic and other) which are specifically quoted as such in Arabic"[13]. In answer to the question: "Why was Mungu not replaced by Allah?," Topan speculates that this is "probably related to the existence of a notion, or concept, of godhood among the Swahili and their neighbours prior to the introduction of Islam at the coast".[14] Topan adds that "perhaps feelings of closeness and intimacy evoked by this indigenous term explain its retention even after the appearance of the Arabic Allah".[15]

Mungu, then, is a common Bantu term for God. Some other Bantu languages use a variant form, i.e. Mulungu. This term or its variant is common, for example, among the Chewa of Malawi, Digo of Kenya, Bena of Tanzania, Pokomo of Kenya, the Kamba of Kenya and the Gogo of Tanzania, among others. Mungu or Mulungu is believed to be the creator and sustainer of the world and of all life in it. This conception is more in terms of personhood rather than of gender. Bantu names and pronouns do not specify gender—masculine, feminine or neutral. They only specify whether the reference belongs to any of the eight or so nominal or semantic classes. For example, the first nominal class, i.e. the M-WA class, consists mainly of persons or people, while the second nominal class, i.e. the KI-VI class, consists mainly of things. It is of interest that in Kihehe, a major Bantu language spoken aroung Iringa, Tanzania, the name for God, Inguluvi, falls into the KI-VI class, i.e. the class of things. But the Wahehe also speak of Inguluvi in terms of personhood,

---

[11] F. M. Topan, "Swahili as a religious language", *Journal of Religion in Africa*, Vol. XXI/4 (1992), 335.

[12] *Ibid.*, 335.

[13] *Ibid.*, 335–336.

[14] *Ibid.*, 336.

[15] *Ibid.*, 336.

as when they refer to God as Magava (the giver), Munyakugada (the creator) or as Maseto (the merciful). The Wahehe thus fluctuate in their God-talk between referring to God as person and God as thing.

Idowu Bolaji and John Mbiti[16] as well as others have amply demonstrated that atheism was unknown in African societies and that the African concept of God was essentially a monotheistic one.[17] While some observers have noted polytheistic or pantheistic elements in African religions,[18] a majority of scholars have been led by the weight of evidence to use a hierarchical model to describe the structure of African religions. They place the supreme being at the apex of the system, followed by various divinities or spirits in decreasing order of power. These are in turn followed by humans and nature. Humans nevertheless retain a privileged place at the centre of this system. The system has been described as in many respects anthropocentric. The divinities in this system have been explained as manifestations or personifications of the supreme being's activities.

However, in the case of the Iraqw the question still arises: why was it necessary to borrow the name of God from the Swahili? Borrowing the name of God from another language is uncommon in East Africa. I have encountered only one other example, in north-eastern Zaire, where the missionary translators following a mission board decision decided to borrow Mungu (God's name in Swahili) for use by the Alur of north-eastern Zaire. The Alur are a Nilotic group also found in Uganda. The Uganda Alur and their Zaire counterparts are essentially one people only separated by an artificial border! The missionaries who worked on this problem in Zaire found the local deity objectionable and not suitable to be taken as a starting point. They concluded that the local deity, as they were led to understand on the basis of their observations and preconceptions, had more in common with the devil than with the God of the Bible as they understood it. Interestingly, on the Ugandan side of the border the deity rejected in Zaire was adopted for use in the church and in the Alur-Uganda Bible, but not in the as yet unfinished Alur-Zaire Bible translation. The latter preferred the Swahili Mungu!

It should be noted that in general the use of God's name in the indigenous language and culture has helped to develop a strong point of contact between the new faith and the traditional indigenous faith. It provides continuity and a basis for the contextualisation and Christianisation of existing forms and beliefs—adding, subtracting or changing them as necessary. It makes possible a less traumatic transformation of the old and an easier transition to the new.

---

[16] See J. Mbiti, *Concepts of God in Africa* (London: S.P.C.K., 1970).

[17] *Ibid.*, 29.

[18] K. van der Jagt, "Equivalence of Religious Terms Across Cultures: Some Problems in Translating the Bible in the Turkana Language," in *Bridging the Gap. African Traditional Religion and Bible Translation* (eds. P. C. Stine and E. R. Wendland; Reading: United Bible Societies, 1990), 131–150 (particularly 140).

God's name in Kiswahili, i.e. Mungu, grafted or transplanted into the Iraqw linguistic religious space has not caught on, despite years of its presence in the area, and despite the attempt to popularise it in the language, culture and faith of the Iraqw-speaking Christians. That Mungu is male or masculine has not helped, given that the devil is believed to be masculine in contrast to the feminine God. The devil is given the name Neetlangw. It is he who has to be placated through sacrifice. Neetlangw, the chief evil being, is the one who demands the blood of cattle, goats and sheep, or he would avenge himself on the people. He is the cause of evil. He is assisted by male spirits referred to as Gi'i. "Gi'I" is generally understood to be the living dead or the "spirits" of the forefathers. Some of these are considered to be evil in the Iraqw world-view.

As already indicated, in the Iraqw language and culture God's name is believed to be Looa. Looa, in opposition to Neetlangw, is believed to be loving and kind. She is the provider, the protector, the merciful, the giver of life. She is the creator, the giver of children and blessings. She is light. She is the sun. She watches over all. She is opposed to darkness. She is the one every Iraqw prays to for protection. She is the one dear to the heart of every Iraqw. She is the one on the lips of every Iraqw, Christian or non-Christian, at a time of danger. The primordial cry in a time of danger is "Ayi[19] ee a Looa", i.e. "O God, my mother." The borrowed Kiswahili term Mungu has not been contextualised or indigenised. Mungu is still a book affair, a Christian liturgy affair. He is not in the everyday life of the people. Iraqw Christians do not evince or express strong feelings of closeness or endearment to God's name in Kiswahili in the environment of their own language and culture. The foreign name does not carry as much moral power or force as does the indigenous name within the general Iraqw social culture space.

At a reviewer's seminar for Old Testament translation in 1990 that was organised in Haydom, Mbulu, a number of Iraqw Christian leaders and pastors were invited for consultation on this matter. It was clear that most of them were not happy with the choice for the Kiswahili Mungu. Many strongly pleaded for a change in official church usage from Mungu to God's name in Iraqw, i.e. from Mungu back to Looa. One leading Christian woman and teacher at the Waama Lutheran Bible School in Mbulu stated that she had found it very difficult to do her evangelical work using God's name in Kiswahili. She claimed that, on the contrary, it was much easier to evangelise and discuss religious matters with non-Christian Iraqw when God's name is used in Iraqw. One Lutheran priest in the Karatu area of Iraqw country is said to have rebelled by maintaining or persisting in the use of Looa in his preaching and teaching. At a translation workshop discussion in October 1993, which included some leading Iraqw Lutheran Christians, there was a strong expression of the need to go back to the use of Looa by the Iraqw Christian churches. Some strongly felt that the next sections of the Old Testament that were to be be printed, namely Genesis and Ruth, should use God's name in Iraqw. It was

---

[19] "Ayi" in Iraqw refers only to one's own mother.

suggested that this should be done on an experimental basis, even though the overwhelming feeling was that this experiment would receive an enthusiastic and positive response from the majority of the Iraqw-speaking Christians.

The objections from some of those who did not favour this proposal were mainly two-fold. The first objection is that Looa is believed to be feminine, whereas the Christian God is believed to be masculine. He is the Father of our Lord Jesus Christ. He is depicted in masculine anthropomorphic imagery. How does one overcome this long tradition of usage? How does one deal with the strong masculine and patriarchal imagery of the Judaeo-Christian Scriptures. Secondly, Looa has strong associations with the sun. It is even possible that some identify Looa with the sun, or think that the sun is Looa.[20] This is partly because the sun is also called looa. Some Christians think that this association is a negative factor or even a distortion of the biblical monotheistic idea which places God the Creator above every created thing, emphasising his transcendent nature. But not everyone accepts the identification theory, i.e. that the sun and God the Creator are identical.

There is no doubt that the Iraqw see Looa as the supreme God. The sun is understood to be only a symbol of the supreme God. It is not itself God but God's eye. According to Mbiti,[21] the sun metaphor is common to many African peoples who see the sun as God's "Great Eye." Among these are the Akan, the Balase, the Galla, the Hadya, the Nandi, the Ovambo or Sidamo. The traditional Iraqw pray facing the sun every morning asking for blessings and long life. This is considered symbolic. Mbiti concludes: "I have not come across any clear indication that the sun is considered to be God or God to be the sun. As our evidence shows, different peoples personify the sun, others take it to be a manifestation of God, and others closely associate it with him".[22]

The objection to the use of Looa based on the gender argument appears to be the only major obstacle. How can it be dealt with, given the strong tradition of Christian male chauvinism and patriarchy? We will do well to remember Gabriel Satiloane's remarks: "What we cannot buy in Western theology is its inevitable dependence on Western culture, civilisation, or whatever you call it. Its Greek-Roman thought-forms and modes of expression are the swaddling clothes that we need to tear open in order to get to Christ.... If theology is reflection, in African theology we try to break the seal of Western thought-forms so that we can come face to face with Christ, in him see ourselves and others."[23] Robert Hood[24] agrees

---

[20] H.-E. Hauge, "Loa, the Sun-Deity of the Iraqw People," in *Temenos* 7 (1971), 50–57.

[21] Mbiti, *Concepts of God in Africa*, 94

[22] *Ibid.*, 134. See also A. Shorter, "African Religions," in *A Handbook of Living Religions* (ed. J. R. Hinnells; Harmondsworth, Middlesex: Penguin Books, 1984), 425–438 (particularly 428).

[23] G. Setiloane, quoted in R. E. Hood, *Must God Remain Greek? Afro Cultures and God Talk* (Minneapolis, Minn.: Augsburg Fortress, 1990), 124–125.

[24] *Ibid.*, 124.

with the above when he observes that: "Traditional Christian doctrines and the theological formation of missionary Christianity both display what can be described as the Graeco-Roman legacy, which is a primary feature of European and American ethnocentric church cultures. This legacy, especially perpetrated in such fundamental doctrines as the Trinity, the two natures of Christ, the work of the Holy Spirit, the concept of sin and salvation, and the division of flesh and spirit, in effect has become a kind of orthodox monoculture that has been universalised as litmus test for Christianity in the third World." It is perhaps the above influence and theological heritage which has contributed to the rejection of the idea of God as mother or God as female. The problem or central question here is whether this dominant tradition merely represents a metaphorical, linguistic or anthropomorphic way of speaking, or whether it defines an ontological distinction. What does it mean to say that God is male or that God is female? Is God a he or a she? Or is God an it (as in Hehe)? What are the distinctive characteristics of each of the above gender categories? Do all of them or just some of them apply to God? The debate on religious language is an old and complex one in the Graeco-Roman, Judaeo-Christian traditions, and has often universalised or absolutised non-essentials to justify the prejudices or biases or the reigning social-cultural or politico-economic ideology.

It is now generally agreed that religious language is essentially metaphorical and is often used in an analogical sense. Literal understandings of key religious metaphors or pictures are bound to lead to distortions of faulty theological systems. What is fundamental or basic to such a metaphor is not the literal picture itself but its essential meaning. The picture itself may be the product of a certain period, a certain society, certain circumstances, but the central meaning of the picture may transcend these realities. A new picture or metaphor may be necessary to recapture the same essential meaning for another period, another society or other sets of circumstances, if such meaning is to retain validity or relevance.

Such is the problem with the metaphor of fatherhood in capturing the essential nature of the supreme being. The idea of God as mother is not limited to the Iraqw. A number of other African peoples share it. Mbiti[25] notes that "The southern Nuba who have a matrilineal system of descent refer to God as 'the Great Mother' and speak of him (her) in feminine pronouns." They say "God gave birth to the world, earth" or that "God as a mother gives birth to, nurtures, cares for, nurses, brings up, protects, etc. her children." The Ovambo of Namibia, who are also matrilineal, say "The mother of people is God." In the Iraqw world-view fatherhood is a metaphor for the dark side of existence. Fatherhood is connected with evil, destruction, death, vengeance, darkness. Thus Neetlangw, the supreme evil being, is conceived in terms of fatherhood. He is the father of evil. He is taata Neetlangw, father Neetlangw. Motherhood, on the other hand, is connected with light. Looa is the sun. She is light. She is Ayi Looa, mother Looa.

---

[25] Mbiti, *Concepts of God in Africa*, 92–93

The biblical metaphors are similarly bound up to their time and place. The essential truths and meanings of course transcend the social situations and times of their origin. It is true that the biblical writings generally depict God in masculine terms. This is a clear reflection of the dominant patriarchal and male chauvinist Near Eastern world-view.

Nevertheless, there are pointers in the biblical writings that the metaphor of God as Father is not monolithic. Both the Hebrew Bible and the New Testament use the metaphor of God as mother. For example, in Isa 49:13–15 we read as follow:

> 13 Sing for Joy, O heavens and exult, O earth;
> break forth, O mountains, into singing!
> For the Lord has comforted his people,
> and will have compassion on his afflicted.
> 14 But Zion said, "The Lord has forsaken me,
> my Lord has forgotten me."
> 15 Can a woman forget her sucking child,
> that she should have no compassion
> on the sons of her womb?
> Even these may forget,
> Yet I will not forget you. (RSV)

Here the Lord is using the metaphor of an earthly mother to convey the depth and power of Her compassion. It should be noted here that the Hebrew word for womb and that for compassion are directly related. The latter is used in a metaphorical and secondary sense, thus drawing its power from the primary imaginary and power of the former, i.e. a mother's womb.

In the New Testament Jesus uses a related image or metaphor, namely that of a mother hen. For example, we read in Matt 23:37–39 (or Luke 13: 34–34) as follows:

> 37 O Jerusalem, Jerusalem, Killing the prophets and stoning those who are sent to you! How often would I have gathered your children together as a hen gathers her brood under her wings, and you would not! 38 Behold your is forsaken and desolate. 39 For I tell you, you will not see me again, until you say, "Blessed is he who comes in the name of the Lord. (RSV)

The mother hen is used here as a metaphor for motherhood in general. There can be no doubt that this metaphor captures best our notions of God's mercy and compassion, her care and protection, or her love and forgiveness.

This is not to say that metaphors of God as father do not convey fundamental and basic truths. The point is that both are metaphors, linguistic pictures, necessarily grounded and bound in time and space, and in specific historical cultures, subject to the vicissitudes of human cultural and linguistic change.

Nevertheless it could be pointed out that the truths these metaphors convey are still valid and relevant. How these truths are to be represented, captured, modelled, pictured or communicated is a function of specific cultures and languages.

Clearly our metaphors of God as father, mother, etc. are not in themselves to be identified with truths of an ontological nature. Neither are they meant to be absolute and immutable. They are merely anthropomorphic, analogical ways of talking about God. They transcend themselves and only point at some essential truth about God. They are merely vehicles for the communication of certain truths. We are admittedly over-simplifying a complex issue—perhaps a mystery relating to the very nature of God. The Iraqw traditional concept of God as mother forces us to re-examine our ways of talking about God and perhaps warns us of the dangers of certain forms of cultural absolutism and obscurantism, or even some form of imperialism. It permits us to explore and to admit new and positive metaphors or models, satisfying the criteria of intelligibility, acceptability, relevance, correctness and validity, consistent as well with our view of a just and loving God. The era of globalisation and the acceptance of the widespread promotion of multiculturalism and pluralism are contributing towards the creation of a freer environment for better appreciation of the Iraqw metaphor of God. Moreover, the rise of the global feminist movement and the robust challenge to patriarchy that it presents allows for a just understanding of the nature of God that is gender sensitive.

Our second case study as illustration of the impact of globalisation on Bible translation concerns the issues of purity and taboo.

PURITY/IMPURITY IN THE IRAQW/GORWA SOCIAL SPACE[26]

Introduction

Many Bible translation teams are hesitant to use terminology from certain spheres of their cultural and religious life, especially when those spheres are deemed or thought to be incompatible with the Christian biblical system. This is likely to be a source of problems in translation. Avoidance of appropriate indigenous terms opens the way for a search for foreign borrowings. An example of this problem may be seen in the search by the Gorwa/Iraqw translation team for ways to translate ritual cleanness or uncleanness, purity or impurity in their language. A related problem is the need to distinguish between the pure and the impure, and between the holy and the common or profane (Lev 10:10). Even when the former distinction is made, as has been noted in a number of East African languages including the Iraqw-Gorwa, the pure is often confused with the holy or the impure with the common or profane, i.e. no distinction is made between the pure and the holy. In the research for this

---

[26] This section is based on research originally prepared for and presented at the UBS Triennial Translation Workshop held in Mexico, 8–25 May 1997 and included in the *UBS Bulletin* 182/183 (1997), 53–65.

paper the focus was mainly on how to deal with the pure and the impure within the social and cultural frameworks of the Iraqw and Gorwa. Problems relating to how the holy and the profane are to be understood will need further research. The brief discussion that follows is therefore only a pointer—or alternatively a mere fragment—indicative of some of the complex and deep realities of the Iraqw/Gorwa life-world.

Even though the Iraqw- and Gorwa-speaking peoples are culturally similar in many ways and speak mutually intelligible dialects, the Gorwa (commonly called by outsiders *Wathiomi*) are often distinguished from their Iraqw cousins (commonly called *Wambulu*). The research on which this discussion is based draws mainly on Gorwa data, but it also applies to a great extent to the Iraqw and others in this family. The Gorwa as well as the Iraqw are among the Cushitic-speaking peoples of Tanzania. The Cushitic language cluster in Tanzania includes, apart from the Iraqw and Gorwa, also the Burunge, the Alagwa, the Kw'adza as well as the Maa or Mbugu of Lushoto in the Usambara Mountains.[27]

According to Gorwa folklore, Gorwa country is the very centre of the universe—"Gorwa aa muruungu Looa" (Gorwa country is the navel of God). It is said among the Gorwa that it is here in their land that the Creator *Looa* performed her great works of creation, and eventually produced the jewel of her creation, namely the first humans, the Gorwa! In fact according to the Gorwa, God is a Gorwa, "Looa aa Gortoo". *Homo*, i.e. non-Gorwa peoples, are therefore closely or distantly related to the Gorwa through geographical dispersion, having corrupted or distorted the original traditions given to the Gorwa at the beginning.

The Gorwa idea of ethnic particularity and uniqueness goes back to creation itself. However, the Iraqw are considered by the Gorwa to have the same ancestral roots and hence come from the same stock. The cultural and linguistic affinity of these two communities as well as their similarity with respect to religious belief and practice no doubt reinforces this perception. Edward H. Winter probably had this in mind when he noted: "The Iraqw, who differ sharply from all other peoples, with one exception, with whom they are in contact in language and in most other aspects of culture, have a very lively awareness of their distinctiveness and of their identity as a single people. Furthermore, the individual has a feeling of loyalty towards the entire people".[28]

In a number of translation-checking sessions Iraqw/Gorwa translators and reviewers assured me that no suitable or appropriate word existed in the

---

[27] See for example C. Ehret, *The Historical Reconstruction of Southern Cushitic Phonology and Vocabulary* (Berlin: Dietrich Reimer Verlag, 1980); F. Nordbustad, *Iraqw Grammar. An Analytical Study of the Iraqw Language* (Berlin: Dietrich Reimer Verlag, 1988).

[28] E. H. Winter, "Territorial Groupings and Religion among the Iraqw,"in *Anthropological Approaches to the Study of Religion* (ed. M. Banton; London: Tavistock Publications, 1966), 161.

Iraqw/Gorwa tongue for the biblical concept of ritual cleanness/uncleanness or purity/impurity. After some prodding about the traditional Iraqw/Gorwa system, the elders agreed that within that system there were indeed powerful and well-known concepts for ritual pollution, uncleanness or impurity. They did not, however, see how these concepts could be used in their Bible. For them the biblical world appears far removed from the Iraqw/Gorwa world. How can one use concepts from the world of darkness for concepts in the world of light? Would one not risk the danger of leading the children of light back to darkness? Doesn't the danger lurk of understanding light in terms of darkness, or more specifically of imposing the Iraqw/Gorwa traditional system onto the Christian biblical system? The Iraqw/Gorwa Christian elders were openly afraid of the ensuing danger of syncretism.

Some Related Pioneer Studies

In exploring concepts of ritual pollution and impurity in the Iraqw/Gorwa social world, one could hardly find a better starting point than that ultimate or most dangerous pollution caused by direct or indirect contact with death. In 1936 E. C. L. Lees brought this problem to the attention of the outside world in a brief and sketchy paper, "A Note on the Wambulu", i.e. the Iraqw, in *Tanganyika Notes and Records* (1936).[29] From his experiences with some of his Iraqw porters who had been bereaved, he wrote:

> I learned later that among the non-Christian Wambulu, tribal custom demands the isolation of near relatives when a death occurs; this continues for a year and, in cases of death from particularly serious diseases, it extends to two years. No one dare go near the afflicted house, which is allowed to become dilapidated and is eventually used as *kuni* (fire-wood) when the ban is raised. For this reason the Wambulu do not build their habitations in villages or even small groups of houses, but spread their dwellings in single units over a wide area; this is no doubt a convenient custom as, if houses were built in close proximity to one another, a death would probably result in the evacuation and eventual destruction of a whole village.

In 1966 Edward H. Winter, also drew attention to the same problem in his paper "Territorial Groupings and Religion among the Iraqw". He wrote:[30]

> As a result of certain events, individuals contract states of ritual impurity: when a man dies, his wife becomes impure; when a woman gives birth to an illegitimate

---

[29] E. C. L. Lees, "A Note on the Wambulu", *Tanganyika Notes and Records* 35 (1936), 106–107. See also C. B. Johnson, "Some Aspects of Iraqw Religion", *Tanzania Notes and Records* 65 (1966), 53–56.

[30] Winter, "Territorial Groupings and Religion", 165.

child, she becomes impure; when a man is clawed by a leopard, he becomes impure. For each of these states the Iraqw have a separate word. When an individual contracts one of these states of impurity, his well-being, indeed his life, is in jeopardy. It is the earth-dwelling spirits who are disturbed by these states of ritual impurity and they are the ones whom an individual fears. A purification ceremony, which usually involves the sacrifice of a sheep or a goat, must be held. After this has taken place the individual must remain in seclusion for a period which may vary from a few days to a year depending upon the type of ritual impurity involved. The reason for this is that once the purification rite has taken place, the person constitutes a danger to others, since the ritual impurity which is leaving him may be contracted by other people if they should come into contact with him.

Mark Bura's 1974 paper[31] on concepts of causation, diagnosis, and treatment of disease among the Iraqw touches on the idea of impurity and its dangers to one's wellbeing. Bura's view is from within, as he is himself Iraqw. His paper written from the perspective of ethnomedicine or medical anthropology and aetiology is illuminating and makes very good reading. Bura, who is a medical doctor, expanded on this earlier paper in his 1984 dissertation for a postgraduate diploma in tropical child health presented to the University of Liverpool's School of Tropical Medicine.[32] This work endeavoured to show how traditional Iraqw taboos and beliefs impact on individual as well as community health, with a specific focus on pregnancy and child-rearing.

It is, however, John Ng'aida's paper "The Concept of Taboo 'meta'[33] among the Iraqw Peoples and Its Hindrances to Christianity"[34] which throws much light on this problem. John Ng'aida is himself Iraqw and hence focuses on the Iraqw in his treatment of the problem. His data are based exclusively on the Iraqw and he naturally draws on his life and experiences in this community. The preface to his study is striking. He writes:

---

[31] M. W. T. Bura, "The Wairaqw concepts of causation, diagnosis and treatment of disease," *Dar es Salaam Medical Journal* 6 (1974), 55–61.

[32] M. W. T. Bura, *Pregnancy and Child-Rearing Practices among the Wairaqw of Tanzania*, a thesis presented for a diploma in tropical child health at the University of Liverpool School of Tropical Medicine, 1984. See also W. D. Kamera, *Tales of the Wairaqw*, (Nairobi: East African Literature Bureau, 1976); W. D. Kamera, "Marmo and Haragasi: Iraqw Folk Theatricals", *African Study Monographs* 4 (1983), 107–118; and W. D. Kamera, "Loo Ammohhuuma—An Iraqw Reconciliation Rite", *Anthropos* 81 (1986), 137–149.

[33] The concept of *meta* (Iraqw) is synonymous with the concept of *tsumi* (Gorwa), which is our main concern in this section.

[34] J. Ng'aida, "The concept of Taboo - 'meta' among the Iraqw peoples and its hindrances to Christianity", Unpublished research paper prepared for Makumira Theological Seminary, Usa River, Arusha, (1975), 1–77.

For many years ever since the 1930s, when Christianity was brought to the Iraqw people, most of the missionaries have neglected the study of the peoples' practices, such as 'meta' - taboo. I have discovered, that 'meta' has been, and it still is, one of the great obstacles to the acceptance of the Christian faith and its propagation, this was because it is a psychological matter which has created an inherent fear in the Iraqw society as a whole. As it has some ethical values to the life of the society, it cannot be simply abandoned. Thus since 'meta' hampers the evangelistic work and the acceptance of the faith, it is something to be taken into consideration seriously.

Ngaida's attempt to think out the implications of this problem for his society is certainly important. He poses a challenge to his people: "We as clergymen and lay Christians have got to know what the 'meta' means to the life of the society, to whom the Gospel is being brought and preached."[35]

Ng'aida goes on in this study to describe the various kinds of taboos in Iraqw society and their consequences. He describes taboos connected with the birth of a child—pregnancy, delivery, naming, weaning, and the case of illegitimate babies; taboos connected with death—death of a child, a youth, a husband, a wife, old people, and the case of suicide; taboos connected with sacrifices, both communal and individual; and taboos on domestic animals. Violation of these taboos leads to communal and personal pollution or uncleanness and consequently to the isolation and exclusion of the violator from the community while he or she is in this state. Purification rites as well as isolation from communal and social life for a certain prescribed period are required to restore those who are unclean. This paper is very informative and reliable. Its author, who was at the time of writing his paper a theological student at the Makumira Theological Seminary, Usa River, Arusha, had a special concern with getting the church to come to terms with this problem, especially with its implications for evangelism and church growth. My contribution here, however, focuses exclusively on understanding the death taboo from a translational perspective, drawing mainly on Gorwa data.

Death-Related Pollution/Uncleanness

Fear of death (*Gwa'araa*) but especially of human corpses (*tuu'aa*) reigns supreme in the Iraqw/Gorwa world. Contact with death or with a human corpse, its remains or a grave is believed to be a cause of uncleanness or social pollution. Such contact with death or death-related subjects is a taboo believed to bring about communal and personal pollution. This state of uncleanness or pollution is referred to as *tsumi*. *Tsumi*, however, refers not only to uncleanness or pollution caused by violation of the death taboo as outlined below, but also to the uncleanness caused by violation of other taboos. This term *tsumi* is also used to refer to the idea of a taboo. Furthermore, a violation of any taboo leads to uncleanness, *tsumi*. The two

---

[35] *Ibid.*, 1.

concepts are therefore almost synonymous to the Gorwa/Iraqw mind. Thus any violation of *tsumi* leads to exclusion or isolation from one's community and turns a normal person into an impure, unclean person, an exile from the social world, a *hé tsumuút*, i.e. one who is *tsumi*. A *hé tsumuút* is so in a double sense—in being both unclean and being taboo, an untouchable social outcast as long as he or she is in that state.

According to the Gorwa/Iraqw traditional belief system, if someone dies inside a house, that house becomes polluted *(tsumi)*. Those dwelling in it also become polluted. Everything in that house also becomes polluted—furniture, clothes, utensils, all foodstuffs—grains, meats, etc. Such a house must be abandoned and left to go to ruins. It is a *dír tsumitá koom*, i.e. an unclean or polluted place. However, fruit trees or green crops around that house are not polluted. Neither are live animals, except those being milked. Their milk is polluted for rest of that milking period. They are not to be milked and no-one can drink or use their milk!

A woman in a *tsumi* state is only so until her pregnancy, i.e. pregnancy terminates her *tsumi* state as she then becomes a bearer or carrier of life and not death. In the case that a woman who is a *hé tsumuút* becomes pregnant, it is assumed that the woman conceived before her *tsumi* state, as during this state no sexual or other normal contacts are lawful. It is interesting to note that a woman who loses her husband is required by these rules to destroy or get rid of all her clothing and adornments. All the bereaved are also required to shave off their hair. The barber in this case should preferably be a resident or non-resident stranger, that is, a foreign non-member of the community, a *homo*. It is the *homo* or foreigner who is often called upon to assist with the disposal of the dead. If this is not possible, then the closest kin, i.e. a spouse or close blood relative such as a parent, brother or cousin, have to bear the awesome responsibility. There are no public funerals in this society, only private disposal of corpses.

The polluted or unclean person is normally isolated, excluded from communal life and activity, and is often forced to physically migrate from the community and seek refuge in an outside community. Such a state of separation or exclusion from the community for death-related reasons is referred to as *xawii*, and the excluded person is a *hé xawaá*. The *hé xawaá* is required to disclose his or her *tsumi* state to elders in the place of refuge, who will treat him or her in accordance with their rules.

The fear that a stranger may be a *hé xawaá* leads to much caution and suspicion of strangers for fear that one may unwittingly violate a taboo and so incur the wrath of the ancestors or unknowingly bring upon oneself some misfortune.

How is the *tsumi* condition formally terminated or brought to an end? Or how is the *hé tsumuút* restored back to the community? The initiative is normally taken by any neighbour who is a member of the community (*inslaawmo*) after the end of the *xawii*, i.e. formal period of exclusion. The neighbour is usually supported or advised by the elders of the community. The restoration includes a water purification ceremony, a *hamtlitoo* generally referred to as *baa/i kwakha*. The water of purification is normally fetched by male elders and not by young people or women, as would normally be the case. In the case of a widow or widower the purification process includes ritual sexual intercourse (*hhehhees*). In the case of the widower the *hhehhees* is with a non-Gorwa/Iraqw i.e. *homo*, and in the case of the widow the *hhehhees* is with a brother-in-law who inherits her. It is the role of the neighbour to invite the remaining head of the house (*aakódo*), or the inheritor of the house (*aaluusmo*) to participate in public social drinking and common eating in the community to formally accept the *hé tsumuút* back to the community. The public restoration and acceptance of the remaining head of the family in this way covers and includes members of his family, of whom he is a representative.

The killing or murder of a stranger (*homo*), i.e. a non-Gorwa/Iraqw, does not lead to *tsumi*. The murderer may, however, need to undergo a purification ritual for shedding blood. But the killing of a fellow Gorwa/Iraqw leads to a much more serious *tsumi* state referred to as *lo'oo*. Such a murderer of a fellow Gormo/Iraqw, *he lo'ór koom*, automatically excludes himself or herself from the community until the relevant purification rites have been performed and other requirements are satisfied. He or she is not to greet anyone. He or she is not to marry while in this state. In fact this crime creates enmity between the murderer's family and the deceased's family. The Iraqw/Gorwa case allows for mediation and the payment of an acceptable fine or recompense as prescribed in order to terminate the state of enmity and restore peace.

Death-related Pollution in Numbers 19 Viewed in the Gorwa/Iraqw Context

How does this impact on Bible translation into Gorwa/Iraqw? G. H. Gray has in his commentary on Numbers[36] correctly pointed to the antiquity and general spread of practices or beliefs concerning death-related pollution or impurity. Thus he writes: "The belief or doctrine underlying the law and the specific regulations here enforced are not, however, necessarily of the same origin and age. The doctrine is this—a dead body is a source or cause of pollution; and this doctrine is both ancient and widespread. There is nothing peculiarly Hebrew, or even peculiarly Semitic about it."[37] He adds "Clearly, then, there is nothing in any way peculiar to the Hebrews in the belief that a dead body is a cause of pollution."[38] Gray cites cases of this practice among the North American Navajo, among the Basuto and Zulu of Southern Africa, the Tibetans, the Madang of Borneo, etc. to show its prevalence in Africa, the Americas, and in the Asia-Pacific region.

The prevalence of the notion of pollution or impurity among many disparate peoples and cultures is clearly a help in promoting a common understanding as well

---

[36] G. H. Gray, *International Critical Commentary on Numbers* (Edinburgh: T&T Clark, 1903).
[37] *Ibid.*, 243.
[38] *Ibid.*, 244.

as in translation across cultures and languages. A close comparison, for example, of the Iraqw/Gorwa system with the ancient Hebrew system as described in Num 19:1–22, indicates that the two systems share quite a number of common elements. A quick look at the Num 19 account reveals that like the Gorwa/Iraqw system, the Hebrew system holds that death-related ritual pollution or uncleanness is brought about by contact with any corpse (Num 19:11, 13), contact with any human remains from a corpse or a human grave (Num 19:16), contact with anyone who has been in contact with a corpse, or in contact with any human remains from a corpse or in contact with a human grave (Num 19:16, 22), contact with any material thing belonging to anyone in any of the above categories (Num 19:22), entering the house or residence of anyone in any of the above categories (Num 19:14, 22), sharing food or drink or just fellowship with such a person (Num 19:20, 22 and by implication from the foregoing). It is to be noted, though, that in the Israelite or Hebrew system in contrast to the Gorwa/Iraqw, loss of a family member—husband, wife, parent, child, brother or sister—does not of itself render one unclean unless one violates the rules indicated above (Num 6:1–12, esp. 6–7, Lev 21:1–15, esp. 11).

It is evident from the foregoing that both the Gorwa/Iraqw system and Israelite/Hebrew system share the concept of pollution and impurity, and that both systems hold that this state has a number of causes including direct or indirect contact with death or anything closely connected to it. Both see pollution or impurity as a threat to the social order and hence seek to exclude the impure or the unclean from the community. Both see the pollution or impurity as affecting not just physical spaces but also people inhabiting those spaces (Num 19:14). Varying periods of exclusion from the community or the duration of the exclusion from the community are prescribed depending on the nature and degree of impurity or uncleanness. Both the Iraqw/Gorwa system and the Hebraic system prescribe rituals or ceremonies of purification to restore those who are impure and have been excluded from the community. In both systems water is an essential element of the purification rituals.

Clearly both systems have the same end in view, namely to maintain purity in the community and so safeguard the community from threats arising from the contrary condition. Mary Douglas has put it this way: "Uncleanness or dirt is that which must not be included if a pattern is to be maintained. To recognise this is the first step towards insight into pollution,"[39] or as is intimated in the title of Douglas's text, impurity and chaos or impurity and danger are closely related. Purity safeguards against danger to the community and to the individual. Impurity and pollution may engender social disintegration and chaos or collapse in the absence of appropriate remedial measures as required. Society must safeguard itself from this danger.

---

[39] M. Douglas, *Purity and Danger. An Analysis of the Concepts of Pollution and Taboo* (London and New York: Ark Paperbacks, 1966, 1984), 40.

Jacob Milgrom held in a critique of Douglas that her "theory of dirt has proved helpful but inadequate; it throws light on the animal classification of Lev. 11, but does not explain it. Far more useful, however, is Douglas's utilisation of the Durkheimean hypothesis that the classification of animals reflects society's values."[40] Here Milgrom probably has in mind Douglas's suggestion in her book *Natural Symbols* (1973)[41] that:

> The first logical categories were social categories; the first classes of things were classes of men into which these things were integrated. It was because men were grouped and thought of themselves in the form of groups that in their ideas they grouped other things. The centre of the first scheme of nature is not the individual; it is society (Durkheim and Mauss). The quest for natural symbols becomes by the force of the argument the quest for natural systems of symbolizing. We will look for correlations between the character of the symbolic system and that of the social system.

In her earlier classic *Purity and Danger* (1966),[42] Douglas expressed the same idea differently as follows:

> The body is a model which can stand for any bounded system. Its boundaries can represent any boundaries which are threatened or precarious. The body is a complex structure. The functions of its different parts and their relations afford a source of symbols for other complex structures. We cannot possibly interpret rituals concerning excreta, breast milk, saliva, and the rest unless we are prepared to see in the body a symbol of society and to see the powers and dangers credited to social structure reproduced on the human body.

Baruch Levine has suggested that "the hidden agenda of Numbers 19 is the cult of the dead". [43] Cults of the dead are understood, according to Levine, as involving "propitiation for the dead through sacrifice and other forms of ritual activity, as well as by magic". They are further "aimed at affording the dead what they seek, namely, an agreeable afterlife". They also "seek to ensure that the powerful dead will not forget the living and will act benevolently rather than malevolently toward them, especially toward their own descendants." Moreover, according to Levine, "a society or community that celebrates a cult of the dead ancestors considers the dead part of the community and family. Their approval is required for the major decisions of the community and their presence is desired at major events in communal life." Levine notes[44] that:

---

[40] J. Milgrom, *Leviticus 1–16* (New York: Doubleday, 1991), 21.
[41] M. Douglas, *Natural Symbols. Explorations in cosmology*, (Harmondsworth, Middlesex: Penguin Books, 1973), 12.
[42] *Idem, Purity and Danger*, 115.
[43] B. Levine, *Numbers 1–20* (New York: Doubleday, 1993), 472.
[44] *Ibid.*, 472–473.

the priestly program expressed in Leviticus 21 and Numbers 21, and in other biblical sources ..., rejects all of these attitudes. The dead have no power, and they are no longer members of the ongoing community. Their exploits during their lifetimes are a source of inspiration and guidance to their descendants, but the community itself looks forward to the future and consigns ancestors to the realm of memory.

This in itself does not mean that there was no cult of the dead in biblical Israel. Levine argues that there was indeed such a royal cult in biblical Israel which was rejected and opposed in the near exilic and exilic periods as evidenced, for example, in the following texts 2 Kgs 22–23; 2 Chr 16:14; Isa 8:16–22; Jer 34:5; Ezek 43:7–9; Amos 6:10; etc. He writes: "Israelites inevitably engaged in rites that would qualify as worship of the dead, notwithstanding deep-rooted objections from priestly and prophetic quarters."[45]

Is the "hidden agenda", to use Milgrom's expression, of the Gorwa/Iraqw purity rules relating to the dead some kind of objection to the cult of the dead so prevalent in many African societies? The so-called living dead are an important institution of African religious practice. There is no doubt that ancestral spirits are an important factor in the life and practices of the Gorwa/Iraqw. The practice of doing homage to the living-dead or taking them into account with respect to decisions affecting everyday life and the community in general is a necessity if disaster or evil has to be averted from the community as well as from the individual. These spirits have to be placated and their general goodwill toward the community sought. However, it seems evident that among the Gorwa/Iraqw there is a widespread fear not only of the dead, but also a fear of their "ghosts" (*mana*, sg., *manu*, pl.), which are thought to forebode evil. The "ghosts" of the dead are often associated with evil and with the Chief Evil being *Neetlangw*.

Ancestral spirits (*gii*, sg., *gai*, pl.) are also associated with sickness and various calamities. They are therefore held in awe and fear. Nothing should be done to anger them or upset them. Libations and sacrifices are therefore offered to the *gai* as well as to *Neetlangw* mainly intended to placate them and so prevent any evil intentions and thus protect society from terrible calamities. Libations are also intended to keep the *gai* and *Neetlangw* from making any demands on the community and to keep them far away from the community. No one wants to come near these evil-causing beings. It is believed, for example, that if one is unlucky enough to see *mana* (a human ghost), one may become sick or lose the power of speech or even go blind. Interestingly such evil ghosts, *manu* or *gai*, are usually considered to be male!

While it is important to recognise the obvious similarities between the Iraqw/Gorwa system and the biblical Israelite system, it is equally important not to overlook the differences between them. There are certainly differences between the

---

[45] *Ibid.*, 478.

two systems. These differences are, however, not fundamental, especially with respect to death-related pollution. They are minor or peripheral and relate mainly to certain practical and symbolic details. For example, in the Israelite system the water of purification (Hebrew *hdn ym / tafh ym*) has to be mixed with the incinerated ash of a red heifer (Hebrew *hmda hrp*) without defect or blemish and which has never been under a yoke.

It is also interesting that in the Israelite system the loss of a family member as a result of death does of itself render one unclean or *tsumi*. A good example is the high priest or the Nazirite who could still maintain their purity and holy status by not attending the death of family members or relatives (see Num 6:1–12; Lev 21:1–15). In this case the factor of holiness or the idea that there can be a class of people called holy is strange in the Iraqw/Gorwa social space. If we take into account the distinctions present in the Israelite system with respect to this domain, namely the one relating to purity, as in Num 19 or Lev 11–15, and the one relating to holiness as in Lev 17–26, it then becomes evident that this is an area where there are real differences from the Iraqw/Gorwa system, which apparently does not have a clear category of the holy as distinct from the pure.

Implications for Translation

Death-related pollution is only one example of the various types of ritual pollution in both the Israelite and the Iraqw/Gorwa systems. The causes for the pollution may differ but the end result is the state of being impure or unclean, i.e. *tsumi* or *hé tsumúut*. Consequently a passage such as Lev 13:45–46: "The leper who has the disease shall wear torn clothes and let the hair of his head hang loose; and he shall cover his upper lip and cry, 'Unclean, unclean.' He shall remain unclean as long as he has disease; he is unclean; he shall dwell alone in a habitation outside the camp", or its exemplification in Mark 1:40–44 should pose no problem to the Iraqw/Gorwa translator. The word for "unclean" in both the Hebrew Bible and the text of Mark yields easily to the above Iraqw/Gorwa conception of pollution. The religio-cultural similarities make for easy cross-cultural comparisons and translational functional equivalences, at least in this case of impurity. The problem arises when a clearly defined concept of holiness, such as in the Hebrew Bible, is lacking in the target language or culture, or when the term for ritual purity and that for holiness tend to converge almost to the extent of being synonymous. How does one disambiguate here in order to make clear the existing distinctions? Some further research is needed to throw some light on how this problem may be dealt with in the case of the Iraqw/Gorwa.

Swahili language translations such as the traditional *Swahili Union Version* (SUV) or the *Biblia Habari Njema* (BHN) exercise some overriding influence in this region and have influenced a number of local translations. Interestingly, the Swahili translations have not only avoided the use of local terminology, opting for Arabic-based terms, but have also not been as consistent as one would have expected in the use of the chosen terms. Thus the BHN, for instance, refers in Leviticus or in the Mark text mentioned above to the unclean person as *najisi* (Lev 11:39-40; 13:2-3, 45-46) and the clean person as *safi* (Lev 13:6, 16-17). For the act of purifying or cleansing, the term *kutakasa* (Lev 14:2) is used. This is the same term used for the act of making holy; so the holy person is referred to as *mtakatifu* (Lev 11:44-45; 20:24-26), a derivative of *kutakasa*. It is clear that the apparent linguistic distinctions here are superficial and arbitrary. As in many other East African languages, making clear the distinction between the holy and the pure has been no easy task, hence the common and widespread borrowing and use of the Swahili Arabic-based terminology. It may be that a concept of the holy was absent in the life-world of East African peoples.

Holiness in the biblical tradition is inseparably connected to the divine, from whence it issues. Indeed the holy is an extension of the divine nature. Places, persons and things are said to be holy by virtue of their possession or control by the divine being or beings. They are exclusively at the disposal or use of the divine being. Milgrom[46] indicates that the holy is "that which is unapproachable except through divinely imposed restrictions" or "that which is withdrawn from common use". In common parlance the holy is that which is set aside for God's use. More positively, "holiness means not only separation from, but separation in order to. It is a positive concept, an inspiration and a goal associated with God's nature and his desire for man. ... Holiness means *imitatio dei*—the life of godliness. ... Thus the emulation of God's holiness demands following the ethics associated with his nature." In ancient Israelite society the demand for holiness in effect led to a certain bifurcation of the community, between the priesthood and the lay people, or between certain holy places and the rest of the unholy, ordinary space. It would appear that Iraqw/Gorwa society, like most east African societies, did not recognise this bifurcation of reality into the holy and the common. The idea of the holy in the Israelite sense seems to be absent here. The idea of the pure, or more correctly the impure, in the above sense seems to have exercised greater power and was/is the controlling force in the ordering of the Iraqw/Gorwa social order.

This naturally leads us to the question of whether the biblical concept of the holy as outlined above is absent in the Iraqw/Gorwa social space (as in many East African societies). How has it been translated into the vernacular scriptures of this region? Four main trends are evident in the translations surveyed. A number of translations have simply failed to distinguish the holy from the pure. Others have simply borrowed from the terms employed by the leading translation in the area, i.e. Swahili. Swahili in turn turned to Arabic which has a mature and developed tradition as preserved in the Islamic scriptures and writings. Yet others have coined neologisms in the language for the new concept. A fourth and last trend, which is not so common, is the use of the descriptive or explanatory approach in the text, which would allow for the clarification of the distinctions among the four

---

[46] Milgrom, *Leviticus 1-16*, 732.

categories discussed above, the pure and the impure, the holy and the profane. Such an approach is exemplified by TEV's rendering of the term holy as in Lev 10:10 (RSV) as what belongs to God.

In the case of the pure or impure, the Gorwa/Iraqw translation has no need to follow any of the four trends mentioned above. This is a case of congruence or equivalence between the two systems, namely that of the source and receptor cultures as well as texts. The use of indigenous terms should follow as a matter of course. The concept of *tsumi* clearly satisfies all relevant criteria for acceptance. It is now commonly agreed by the Iraqw/Gorwa translation team and its supporting committees that there is no reason why *tsumi* should not be used. What is now needed, however, is another look at the concept of the holy in the light of the Iraqw/Gorwa system, with a view to distinguishing it from the concept of the pure or the clean which has been in focus here. Research is needed to facilitate this. Another obstacle that still needs to be overcome with respect to the Gorwa/Iraqw social system is the tendency to tie Iraqw/Gorwa terms so closely to their traditional belief system that their use in another system such as the Christian biblical system generates shock and cultural confusion. How, in other words, are Iraqw/Gorwa concepts which have unacceptable Christian implications or clash with the Christian ethical system to be christianised or divested and emptied of their negative traditional systemic implications? Clearly this question goes beyond semantics.

CONCLUSION

Interestingly, the resolution to these clashes of belief systems and world views are not being sorted out theoretically, but are rather negotiated in the context of the pressures of modern life and inter-ethnic and inter-cultural contact and mixing, in the context of social change, demographic changes, rural urban migration, rapid economic developments and changes, political and ideological changes, religious conversions, disease epidemics, educational changes and the like. The impact of all these factors has led, and is still leading to, far-reaching changes in the nature of present-day Iraqw/Gorwa society, as in other Tanzanian or African societies. The impact of globalisation on biblical translation is therefore an indirect one: when the values of these African societies transform and change under the influence of a globalised world, the landscape within which Bible translation takes place also changes. On account of the inseparable relationship between translation and the world-view, values and cultural environment of the receptor community, globalisation makes Bible translation a very complex endeavour!

ACKNOWLEDGEMENTS

For information regarding the Iraqw and Gorwa I am greatly indebted to the following members of the Iraqw/Gorwa Old Testament translation project: the Gorwa-speaking team members, Rev. John Nahhato, Rev.Hezekiah Kodi and Mrs Mary Bura; and the Iraqw-speaking team members this project, Rev. Yotham Girgis, Rev. Ibrahim Mathiya, Dr Mark Bura and Ms. Frøydis Nordbustad. They all freely and generously gave me of their time and resources. They allowed me to spend much time with them in lengthy conversations, discussions, and interviews on these issues. I learnt much in the process and wish to take this space to express my gratitude and appreciation to all of them.

Part IV

AFTERWORD

When Biblical Scholars Talk About "Global" Biblical Interpretation

KNUT HOLTER

INTRODUCTION

Once in the late 1990s I was invited to give some lectures at a university in Nairobi. The topic was "contextual Old Testament interpretation", and with the zeal of the newly converted I advocated the necessity of contextual sensitivity—that is sensitivity vis-à-vis the contemporary interpreter's context—in biblical interpretation. Consequently, I tried to draw some lines between the interpretative context of my students, which I assumed to be that of traditional East African culture and religion, and some Old Testament texts and motifs. It should be admitted that I expected my topic to be met with some enthusiasm, as I knew from their biblical studies curriculum that the students were normally exposed to traditional—and I would then and now add "Western"—historical-critical scholarship only. However, the enthusiasm I met was quite moderate, and I had a feeling that the students did not to catch my point.

A colleague in the Religious Studies department explained the whole thing to me. "It's your concept of context", he said. "You take for granted that their interpretative context is found in traditional East African culture and religion, but it is not. These students are almost as far away from traditional African culture and religion as you." And then he outlined the background of the average student in my Old Testament class: metropolis and middle class, Levi's trousers and Nike shoes, McDonald's and Burger King, Michael Jackson and Britney Spears, and not least, being born again in one of the many United States-inspired Pentecostal churches. "With your focus on traditional African culture and religion as interpretative resources for Old Testament interpretation in Africa you probably won't like this", my colleague argued somewhat ironically, "but these students are actually children of the modern globalization."

My encounter with the students in Nairobi a decade ago taught me a couple of things. One is that, due to the multifaceted economic, political and cultural monster called "globalization", someone living in an African metropolis may experience life—and read the Bible—more or less in the same ways as someone living in another metropolis in whatever part of the globe. Another is that the relationship between biblical interpretation as part of the "globalization" project and a more ethically sensitive "global" biblical hermeneutics is at best quite ambivalent. The following is an attempt at elaborating a bit on these insights.

"GLOBALIZATION" AND BIBLICAL INTERPRETATION

There is reason to assume, I think, that contemporary biblical interpretation is part of the modern globalization project from at least two perspectives. First, in the first decade of the twenty-first century, we face a global distribution of communities that interpret the Bible. Historically speaking, the development of Christianity into a *de facto* global religion took place in parallel with—and was in several ways an important exponent of—the Western expansionism towards the end of the second millennium. Nevertheless, whatever the historical causes were, the result was that Christianity throughout the twentieth century changed from being a predominantly Western religion to becoming a global religion, with adherents in nearly "every nation, tribe, people and language."[1] Admittedly, the global distribution of Christian communities is not necessarily identical with the distribution of (lay and professional) interpretative communities for the Bible, as examples of the Bible being embraced and interpreted outside the realms and influences of the church (and synagogue) are gradually being identified.[2] Nevertheless, as far as numbers and general influence are concerned, there is no doubt that biblical interpretation is an activity that predominantly characterizes religious and academic communities related to Christianity.

Second, contemporary biblical interpretation is also part of the modern globalization project in the sense that the mainstream approaches to the Bible that are attested within these globally distributed interpretative communities tend to prolong the traditionally Western hegemony of theological (to some extent) and exegetical (to a larger extent) biblical interpretation. The concepts of biblical interpretation that have been developed throughout the history of church and academia in the West were (and are) consciously and unconsciously exported to their younger counterparts in the rest of the world. Moreover, church and academia in the West are still in the position of having the economic and institutional power to define *proper* interpretation of the Bible, as the following anecdote may illustrate. Once in the mid-1990s I visited a graduate school of theology in Nigeria. The school had inherited the complete library of a theological seminary that had recently been closed down somewhere in the United States: the books, the card catalogue, and even the book shelves and pictures used to decorate the library in the American seminary. The positive effect of this "gift from heaven" (as they saw it)

---

[1] For statistics and references, see my essay in the beginning of this essay collection: "Geographical and institutional aspects of global Old Testament studies".

[2] Cf. G. O. West, "Mapping African biblical interpretation: A tentative sketch," in G. O. West and M. W. Dube (eds.), *The Bible in Africa: Transactions, Trajectories and Trends* (Leiden: Brill, 2000), 29–53; *idem*, "Early encounters with the Bible among the Batlhaping: Historical and Hermeneutical signs", *Biblical Interpretation* 12 (2004), 251–281; G. Razafindrakoto, "The Old Testament outside the realm of the church: A case from Madagascar," in *Let My People Stay! Researching the Old Testament in Africa* (ed. K. Holter; Nairobi: Acton, 2006), 97–110.

was that the Nigerian school got a relatively updated library of ten thousand volumes or so. The negative effect, though, was that the library hardly contained any books that were written from an African perspective, as the school was not able to find room in its annual budget for purchasing more contextually relevant books. The library was (and probably still is) therefore not of much help for lecturers and students aiming to reflect theologically and exegetically in relation to their immediate geographical, social and cultural context. And further, the library gave (and probably still gives) the impression that professional biblical interpretation basically is a Western thing. The *proper* interpretation of the Bible, as it were, is found in theological and exegetical literature written by Western scholars from Western perspectives, and it is eventually stored in bookshelves that are made in the United States and surrounded by beautiful landscape photos from Texas.

In other words, we notice that the consequences of the modern globalization on biblical interpretation point in quite opposite directions; a global distribution of interpretative communities on the one hand, and a continuation of the traditional Western interpretative hegemony on the other. Whether the latter is a problem or not for the former, is a political (hence interpretatively relevant!) question. Many biblical interpreters—not only in the West, even my Old Testament class in Nairobi—do not think of it as such, as they tend to approach biblical interpretation from perspectives that underestimate the role of the interpretative context. Others, however, do find it increasingly problematic that interpretative strategies developed within (and therefore reflecting) Western (male and middle class) experiences are assumed to represent some kind of universality, principally and practically detached from the socio-cultural context of the interpreter.

In response, therefore, a growing number of alternative, or perhaps we should rather say resistant, interpretative strategies have been developed. These strategies are alternative in the sense that they reject the concept of universality of traditional Western interpretation, and they are resistant in the sense that they—from post-colonial, liberationist, feminist, and other consciously ideological perspectives—let their interpretation voice the experiences and concerns of those who are marginalized by the dominant, Western minorities of biblical interpreters.[3] Such alternative or resistant interpretative strategies may for some time have been thought of as "voices from the margins" of the mainstream Western guilds of

---

[3] Cf. e.g. E. Schüssler Fiorenza, *Rhetoric and Ethic: The Politics of Biblical Studies* (Minneapolis: Fortress Press, 1999); G. O. West, *The Academy of the Poor: Towards a Dialogical Reading of the Bible* (Interventions 2; Sheffield: Sheffield Academic Press, 1999); F. F. Segovia, *Decolonizing Biblical Studies: A View from the Margins* (Maryknoll, N.Y.: Orbis, 2000); R. Boer, *Last Stop Before Antarctica: The Bible and Postcolonialism in Australia* (The Bible and Postcolonialism 6; Sheffield: Sheffield Academic Press, 2001); R. S. Sugirtharajah, *Postcolonial Criticism and Biblical Interpretation* (Oxford: Oxford University Press, 2002).

biblical interpretation,[4] but they are now gradually being acknowledged even by these guilds of theology (to some extent) and biblical studies (to a less extent) as representing central, interpretative concerns. Moreover, taken together, such contextually sensitive interpretative strategies are "global", in the sense that they grow out of experiences of "every nation, tribe, people and language."

Contemporary "Global" Biblical Interpretation

Throughout the last decade, several collaborative book projects have put the concept of "global" biblical interpretation on the agenda. A brief look at how the concept is approached in three sets of representative examples from the (more or less) global guild of biblical scholarship would therefore be of interest to us.

A first set of examples is the essay collection *Return to Babel: Global Perspectives on the Bible*, edited by John R. Levison and Priscilla Pope-Levison (1999).[5] The title alludes to the Tower of Babel narrative in Gen 11, interpreting, however, the destruction of the tower and confusion of languages not as a kind of punishment, rather as a signal event in the restoration of a desirable diversity, against the unification project of the Babylonian empire.[6] Diversity is in several ways a key concept in the essay collection, too. Diversity with regard to the personal, cultural, social, geographical, educational, and denominational background of the authors, a diversity they are supposed to bring with them into their encounter with the biblical texts. The book includes thirty essays by fifteen authors, and these authors come from twelve countries in Latin America, Africa and Asia. The essays are systematically gathered and presented in ten chapters, of which five interpret texts from the Old and five texts from the New Testament. In each case, three authors are asked to give an interpretation of the same text, and to explicitly make use of their Latin American, African and Asian contexts as interpretative resources vis-à-vis the text.

An illustrative case is the Tower of Babel narrative in Gen 11, referred to above. From a Latin American perspective, José Míguez-Bonino (Argentina) points to the sixteenth-century Spanish conquest, which included a rejection of all vernacular languages. Against this background, the confusion of languages in Gen 11 may be read as a blessing, preparing for the blessing of all nations in Gen 12.[7]

---

[4] Cf. R. S. Sugirtharajah (ed.), *Voices from the Margin: Interpreting the Bible in the Third World* (Maryknoll, N.Y.: Orbis, 1991); idem (ed.), *Still at the Margins: Biblical Scholarship Fifteen Years after Voices from the Margin* (London: T&T Clark, 2008).

[5] J. R. Levison and P. Pope–Levison (eds.), *Return to Babel: Global Perspectives on the Bible* (Louisville: Westminster John Knox, 1999).

[6] Ibid., 1–2.

[7] J. Míguez-Bonino, "Genesis 11:1–9. A Latin American perspective," in *Return to Babel: Global Perspectives on the Bible* (eds. J. R. Levison and P. Pope-Levison; Louisville: Westminster John Knox, 1999), 13–16.

Further, from an African perspective, Solomon Avotri (Ghana) points to a widespread myth in Africa—the blue bird story—about the double relationship between the Divine and the human beings, a relationship of simultaneous closeness and remoteness. Against this background, the Gen 11 narrative describes a universal experience.[8] Finally, from an Asian perspective, Choan-Seng Song (Taiwan) points to an incident from the Sino-Japanese war in 1895, when five peace-searching Taiwanese brothers in a small fishing village were killed by Japanese soldiers who were not able to understand what they said. Against this background, the Gen 11 narrative encourages its readers to strive towards a community in which "one language and the same words" can be heard in the world of "many languages and different words".[9]

As a whole, this essay collection is a good example of contextual interpretation, from different parts of the globe. Nevertheless, one could have wished that a book on "global perspectives on the Bible" had shown more explicit attention to the book title's key term "global", a term whose geographical connotations seem to be taken for granted. One thing is that the book does not relate this key concept to the current discussion of "globalization". More surprising, though, is it that the book has an implicit understanding of "global" that excludes European and North American interpretative perspectives. If the book was meant to present "voices from the margins", its focus on Latin American, African and Asian perspectives would have been understandable, although a mere geographical understanding of the center/margins relationship hardly is satisfactory any longer. But in a "global" symphony of interpretative experiences and concerns, it is difficult to see the point of totally excluding the Western heritage with the Bible. Although unintended, this may support the outdated idea that only non-Western biblical interpretation is contextual.

A second set of examples is the *Global Bible Commentary*, edited by Daniel Patte *et al.* (2004).[10] The book is a "bible commentary", in the sense that all books in the (Protestant) Bible are approached from isagogic, exegetical, and hermeneutic perspectives. And it is a "global" commentary, in the sense that scholars from (nearly) all over the globe were asked not only to contribute, but also to make use of their own contextual experiences when they approached their assigned biblical book. The meaning of the term "global", however, is here, too, more or less taken for granted. Although gender issues lie under the surface, "global" is mainly a question of geography. Nevertheless, contrary to the previous

---

[8] S. Avotri, "Genesis 11:1–9. An African perspective," in *Return to Babel: Global Perspectives on the Bible* (eds. J. R. Levison and P. Pope-Levison; Louisville: Westminster John Knox, 1999), 17–25.

[9] C.-S. Song, "Genesis 11:1–9. An Asian perspective," in *Return to Babel: Global Perspectives on the Bible* (eds. J. R. Levison and P. Pope-Levison; Louisville: Westminster John Knox, 1999), 27–33.

[10] D. Patte *et al.* (eds.) *Global Bible Commentary* (Nashville: Abingdon, 2004).

example (Levison and Pope-Levison 1999), the term here includes European and North American commentators, as the editors wanted the commentary to reflect the demography of today's readers of the Bible. Hence, of seventy-one commentators, two-thirds come from Africa, Asia, Latin America, and Oceania, and (nearly) half are women.[11]

The commentators have been free to define their own particular context. Some, therefore, emphasize socio-cultural aspects whereas others emphasize more socio-economic aspects. Even though the editorial introduction does not address the issue of globalization as such, some of the commentators touch typical globalization questions. An illustrative example is Jorge Pixley (Nicaragua), who reads Exodus in a socio-economic context of "formal democracies and dramatically declining lifestyles for the majority of the people." "It is a situation", he argues, "dominated by a global market in an era when capitalism is no longer a growing productive force", and the structural explanation of this is found in "a merciless extraction of wealth from impoverished countries, an extraction that is only possible through a policing network of financial organizations controlled by U.S. financial interests", such as the International Monetary Fund, the World Trade Organization, and the World Bank. In such an unjust context, Exodus' revolutionary message about freedom from oppression and the creation of a new society based on just principles may serve as a challenging model.[12]

A third set of examples is the book series "Global Perspectives on Biblical Scholarship", initiated by the Society of Biblical Literature a decade ago, and now with a dozen volumes or so.[13] The first volume in the series grew out from the SBL International Meeting in Helsinki (Finland) in 1999,[14] and it offers an interesting discussion between Heikki Räisänen (Finland) and Elisabeth Schüssler Fiorenza (USA) on the role of the "old paradigm" of historical-critical interpretation in relation to the "new paradigm" of feminist, liberationist, post-colonial, etc. interpretation. Proceeding from Schüssler Fiorenza's famous 1987 SBL Presidential Address on decentering biblical scholarship,[15] Räisänen argues that the "old paradigm" should not be seen as contrary to the "new", rather as an ally. When it has not always been experienced that way, it is not the fault of the method, rather of its practitioners, he argues, programmatically claiming that the "colonial attitude

---

[11] *Ibid.*, xxi–xxxii.

[12] J. Pixley, "Exodus", in *Global Bible Commentary* (eds. D. Patte *et al.*; Nashville: Abingdon, 2004), 17–29, especially 17–18, 28–29.

[13] Cf. J.T. Fitzgerald *et al.* (eds.), *Animosity, the Bible, and Us: Some European, North American, and South African Perspectives* (Global Perspectives on Biblical Scholarship 12; Atlanta: Society of Biblical Literature, 2009).

[14] H. Räisänen *et al.* (eds.), *Reading the Bible in the Global Village: Helsinki* (Global Perspectives on Biblical Scholarship 1; Atlanta: Society of Biblical Literature, 2000).

[15] E. Schüssler Fiorenza, "The ethics of biblical interpretation: Decentering biblical scholarship", *JBL* 107 (1988), 3–17.

is *not* inherent in the historical approach itself."[16] Schüssler Fiorenza, however, is not convinced by Räisänen's defence of the Western interpretative heritage. She sticks to her 1987 claims, arguing "that a decentering of hegemonic biblical scholarship has to take place so that practitioners from different social locations can move into and reconstitute the center of biblical studies."[17]

The subsequent volumes in the series address the quest for "global perspectives" from various thematic and hermeneutical positions: feminist, contextual, post-colonial, etc.[18] One concept that has received some attention is that of the "global village", and the discussion between Justin S. Ukpong (Nigeria) and Musa W. Dube (Botswana) in a volume based on the SBL International Meeting in Cape Town (South Africa) in 2000 is illustrative with regard to how this concept may be approached.[19] In his opening address at the Cape Town meeting, Ukpong argues that the modern globalization in reality continues old colonial patterns. What we commonly refer to as the "global village" is "only a *unidirectional* [Ukpong's emphasis] globalization. It is the extension of Western cultural practices to other parts of the globe with all the good and evil effects that entail."[20] Hence, he continues, with regard to non-Western biblical scholarship, as long as it "is consigned to the margin of biblical scholarship and therefore ignored or treated as of no consequence, we shall be far from living out the global village content."[21] In her response to Ukpong, Dube elaborates some of his major points. Concurring with him that globalization in many ways continues colonization, she emphasizes that even though globalization benefits many, it still leaves many others economically worse off and dehumanized.[22] This has obvious consequences for the

---

[16] H. Räisänen, "Biblical critics in the global village," in *Reading the Bible in the Global Village: Helsinki* (eds. H. Räisänen *et al.*; Global Perspectives on Biblical Scholarship 1; Atlanta: Society of Biblical Literature, 2000), 9–28 and 153–166.

[17] E. Schüssler Fiorenza, "Defending the center, trivializing the margins," in *Reading the Bible in the Global Village: Helsinki* (eds. H. Räisänen *et al.*; Global Perspectives on Biblical Scholarship 1; Atlanta: Society of Biblical Literature, 2000), 29–48 and 166–169.

[18] Cf. e.g. M. W. Dube (ed.), *Other Ways of Reading: African Women and the Bible* (Global Perspectives on Biblical Scholarship 2; Atlanta: Society of Biblical Literature, 2001); C. Van der Stichele and T. Penner (eds.), *Her Master's Tools: Feminist and Postcolonial Engagements of Historical-Critical Discourse*. (Global Perspectives on Biblical Scholarship 9; Atlanta: Society of Biblical Literature, 2005).

[19] J. S. Ukpong, "Reading the Bible in a global village: Issues and challenges from African reading," in *Reading the Bible in the Global Village: Cape Town* (eds. J. S. Ukpong *et al.*; Global Perspectives on Biblical Scholarship 3; Atlanta: Society of Biblical Literature, 2002), 9–39 and 179.

[20] *Ibid.*, 35.

[21] *Ibid.*

[22] M. W. Dube, "Villagizing, globalizing, and biblical studies," in *Reading the Bible in the Global Village: Cape Town* (eds. J. S. Ukpong *et al.*; Global Perspectives on Biblical Scholarship 3; Atlanta: Society of Biblical Literature, 2002), 41–63 and 179–184.

role of biblical studies, she argues, criticizing Ukpong's concept of the global village for ignoring central interpretative experiences, such as gender, race and class.[23]

"GLOBAL" VERSUS "GLOBALIZATION"

These three sets of examples confirm, I think, my assumption (cf. above, II) that contemporary biblical interpretation is part of the modern globalization project from at least two perspectives. The first perspective acknowledges the fact that we today face a global distribution of communities that interpret the Bible, whereas the second perspective acknowledges—and in some cases tries to counteract—the fact that these globally distributed interpretative communities tend to prolong the traditionally Western hegemony of biblical interpretation.

As a whole, the three sets of examples—but also the present essay collection—are dominated by the first perspective. The essay collections edited by Levison and Pope-Levison (1999) and Patte *et al.* (2004) have both attempted to let global—not only in a geographical sense—concerns be voiced. So has the present essay collection, with contributors coming from different geographical and hermeneutical backgrounds. And, certainly, the fact that the Bible now is being interpreted all over the globe, by people of diverse ethnic, gender, cultural, social, geographical, educational, and denominational backgrounds should not be underestimated. For the first time in the history of the church—and the implicit history of the interpretation of the Bible—we face today the existence of a global and democratic biblical readership, as the Bible (or parts of it) is now translated into the languages of ninety to ninety-five percent of the world's population. Translation—as well as distribution and interpretation—of the Bible is a central characteristic of the Christian church.[24] Through the efforts of millions of interpreters, the biblical texts are now being read into (and out of) a global multitude of languages and cultures, with the result that not only all the lay interpreters, but indeed also the professional ones, the members of *our* academic guilds, now "speak in other tongues."[25]

However, the second perspective, too, should get attention, the one that acknowledges—and in some cases tries to counteract—the fact that these globally distributed interpretative communities tend to prolong the traditionally Western hegemony of biblical interpretation. In the present essay collection, this concern is especially voiced by May and Jonker. In the three previous sets of examples, the

---

[23] *Ibid.*, 55.

[24] Cf. L. Sanneh, *Disciples of All Nations: Pillars of World Christianity* (Oxford: Oxford University Press, 2008).

[25] Cf. F. F. Segovia, "'And they began to speak in other tongues': Competing modes of discourse in contemporary biblical criticism," in *Reading from this Place: Social Location and Biblical Interpretation in the United States* (eds. F. F. Segovia and M. A. Tolbert; Minneapolis: Fortress, 1995), 1–32.

concern is expressed most clearly in the SBL series "Global Perspectives on Biblical Scholarship". Biblical interpretation is no innocent activity. The ethical concern raised by Schüssler Fiorenza about a decentering of biblical scholarship requests interpreters that come from different social locations. Ukpong and Dube follow this up; Ukpong, when he points at Western biblical scholarship as part of a unidirectional globalization, and Dube, when she requests a biblical scholarship that includes gender, race, and class as interpretative experiences.

I started this essay with an anecdote from Nairobi. My students were not overly enthusiastic about my focus on traditional East African culture and religion as interpretative resources for Old Testament interpretation. The mistake was of course mine. I had an outdated and too romantic concept of their immediate context. Nevertheless, I still think I had a point, that of the contextual emphasis, the willingness to make use of the students' contextual experiences and concerns as interpretative resources vis-à-vis the biblical texts. The Bible is today interpreted all over the globe by people who consciously make use of their context as interpretative resources. As an irony of fate, it is this global presence of contextual interpretations that is able to balance or even counteract the traditionally Western hegemony on biblical interpretation caused by the modern globalization.

www.ingramcontent.com/pod-product-compliance
Lightning Source LLC
Chambersburg PA
CBHW032303150426
43195CB00008BA/560